GREAT BRAND STO[R]
PREMIUM BONDS

Nice little ERNIE
A 21st century national treasure

Mark Griffiths

CYANBOOKS

For Debs, stan&clan and much
more than average luck

Copyright © 2007 Mark Griffiths

First published in 2007 by Cyan Books, an imprint of

Cyan Communications Limited
119 Wardour Street
London W1F 0UW
United Kingdom
T: +44 (0)20 7565 6120
sales@cyanbooks.com
www.cyanbooks.com

The right of Mark Griffiths to be identified as the author of
this work has been asserted by him in accordance with the
Copyright, Designs and Patents Act 1988.

A CIP record for this book is available from the British Library.

ISBN-13 978-1-904879-07-7
ISBN-10 1-904879-07-1

Book design: So… www.soitbegins.co.uk

Printed and bound in Great Britain by
TJ International Ltd, Padstow, Cornwall

CONTENTS

Happy 50th Birthday Ernie!

Which British financial savings brand has over 23 million customers and sold more product in the last five years than in the previous 45? Holds £35 billion of stock and creates two millionaires every month? Sold £480 million in one month on the Internet alone and has an average sales value of £2,000? Don't tell me you've never heard of it. You probably own some of the product.

Until recently, Premium Bonds were Britain's best-kept secret brand. Yet, since 1956, the government-backed savings scheme cum lottery has been steadily accumulating funds to the extent that over four in ten of us now own Premium Bonds. The odd thing is that some of us don't even know it.

Nobody has ever written a book about Premium Bonds. Lumped in with many financial brands, they're often deemed too boring to pass mention. "You're writing a book about Premium Bonds?!" asked my "Uncle" Vic at my sister's wedding. "How do you even begin?" I think Vic was really trying to tell me that there is not enough to say about Premium Bonds. That is, there's very little interest in them (ha ha!). How wrong he was!

It's important to say that some brands can suffer from over-analysis. Especially when the message is simple, the delivery is straightforward and the whole experience is, well, simple and straightforward. Premium Bonds are such a brand and I have no intention of analyzing all the mystery out of them, though I will try to get underneath their papery skin. Much of my focus is going to be on the culture that produced and sustains Premium Bonds. I think it says more about Premium Bonds than Premium Bonds could possibly say themselves.

You'll have seen the TV ads featuring Sir Alan Sugar. What picture does your mind conjure when I tell you that Premium Bonds were once promoted by Hollywood siren, Jayne Mansfield? Don't know her? Off to Wikipedia with you!

Over the last 50 years, the great British institution known as Premium Bonds has used a varied cast of sugar and spice to persuade Middle Britain to save for a day when the rain stops. We've all been hoping that ERNIE, the number crunching personality at the heart of it all, will produce the big winning ticket.

Premium Bonds marketing has always made a big fuss of ERNIE. I'm happy to join in. ERNIE, you've never blessed me with a penny, but I appreciate what you've done for the British public and the maintenance of our very special culture. Considering where I'm coming from, that's praise indeed. You see, like many of us, I do not trust financial service institutions, particularly since I lost a good part of two pensions with Equitable Life. Yet the view of Premium Bonds I present here is one of warmth and astonishment in equal measure. I didn't know much about Premium Bonds when Cyan Books asked me to write this. I've had to start from scratch in terms of understanding Premium Bonds and gathering the information. I've had a good deal of useful help from various people at parent organization, National Savings & Investments (NS&I), but I've done my own research, voiced my own opinions and come to my own conclusions.

1974 POSTER FEATURING FRANKIE HOWERD

PREMIUM BONDS
New top monthly prize
£75,000

Up your Bonds.
I should say so…

5

From an independent point of view, I can see that Premium Bonds are a personal savings product that needs to be viewed in a wide, social context, a very British social context. In the words of NS&I themselves, "Premium Bonds are a fun yet serious way of saving money," So the way I've written about Premium Bonds illuminates the brand in a fun yet serious light. This is particularly evident in the cultural timeline at the end of the book. Creating this mnemonic touchstone has taught me as much about what British people feel about Premium Bonds as any other aspect of my research. After all, I'm one of them, one of us. I am neither a critic nor a financial expert; I'm looking at a brand and its place in our world – as someone who writes for and about brands, as a consumer in this culture.

As brands don't exist without people and their experiences and opinions, the book is full of personal stories and perceptions – about winners (and non-winners), about punters (and non-players), about commentators (and passers-by). My approach is to be entirely curious about Premium Bonds and National Savings & Investments while taking a challenging and occasionally humorous look at the culture that produced the brand and sustains it. I'll be making lots of cultural allusions and, naturally, these will all be my own, except where the jokes are better.

There are many things I have to say about Premium Bonds. But, in the meantime…

1

BOND FEVER
THE MYSTERY OF BRITAIN'S BEST-KEPT SECRET BRAND

LOOK AT IT THIS WAY

WHEN WAYNE ROONEY IS 34, HOW OLD WILL YOU BE?

Look to the future. Open your eyes to 2020. Have you orbited the planet yet? Richard Branson is our sprightly 70-year-old President of the UK and entrepreneurialism is a compulsory subject on the national curriculum from the age of three. The England football team still hasn't won the World Cup again. Under pressure, 34-year-old England captain, Wayne Rooney, has just notched up 200 caps and teeters on the edge of a new England all-time scoring record of 50 goals. He hasn't scored for five years. The Nigerian Olympic Games have not quite gone as expected. They've come in under budget, featuring exemplary accountability, more successful than any other. Young Britons are moving to China in their droves, where the best-paid jobs are. That schoolboy Mandarin is coming in handy after all!

Get the picture? OK, it isn't the dystopian sci-fantasy world depicted in the 1980s film, *Bladerunner*, although that world is alive and kicking on the Internet. But everything has changed. Hold it there! Not everything. You've still got your Premium Bonds, haven't you?

Actually, the world I've just depicted is not that far away. And just as there is absolutely no foreseeable reason why a veteran Wayne Rooney should not be leading out his England team in a World Cup final, so there is none why you should not still be owning Premium Bonds and buying more.

Have I twisted your neck a little, here? Are you trying to look backwards to your grandparents' era, when I'm compelling you to look forward to a time, and beyond, when you are that age yourself?

PREMIUM BONDS REACH 50 YEARS OLD

What about the present? Never mind *Casino Royale*, 2006 was all about a different type of Bond Fever. When Sir Alan Sugar was promoting the 50th anniversary of the launch of the national institution known as Premium Bonds, the public went wild for the chance to win one of five £1 million prizes on offer in the

December 2006 draw. And then again, in June 2007, upon the anniversary of the first draw itself. That's you, probably.

Want to see a stat? Here's one for you…

In October 2006 alone, you bought £2.2 billion worth of Premium Bonds. Read that again. You thought I said *million*.

Even though your odds of winning a £1 million prize are one person in several Planet Earths.

To appreciate Premium Bonds, you have to see the story in numbers…

Someone buys Premium Bonds every **10** seconds.

Around **40%** of the British public hold Premium Bonds and many customers have a substantial amount of money invested.

Over **23.6** million people hold more than £35 billion bonds.

That means over **35** billion eligible Premium Bonds go into each monthly draw.

The odds of winning a Premium Bond prize are currently **24,000–1**.

350,000 people hold the maximum £30,000 – about 1.5% of all bond holders. With average luck they should win 15 prizes a year.

780,000 holders have £20,000 or more. With average luck they should win 10 prizes a year.

More than **1.75** million people hold £5,000 worth of Bonds. With average luck they should win two to three prizes a year.

If you have just one £1 Premium Bond your auntie bought you as a kid, you've got about a one in **17.5** billion chance of winning one of those two £1 million prizes.

There are currently over **495,000** unclaimed Premium Bond prizes worth over £28 million.

2006 POSTER

Premium Bonds
Anniversary Prize Draws

Premium Bonds
50th anniversary

national savings
& investments

50 ns&i

Five £1 million jackpots

Celebrating 50 years of Premium Bonds with TWO anniversary prize draws, each with FIVE £1 million jackpots

Have you checked your numbers? Every month, National Savings & Investments (NS&I), the Government-backed organization that runs Premium Bonds, gets one million visits to its website from people doing just that. The call centres in Blackpool, Durham and Glasgow receive 13,000 telephone calls every day and more than 3.5 million calls a year.

By 1st May 2007, Premium Bond holders have won more than 152 million tax-free prizes worth a combined total of £9.7 billion since the very first Premium Bonds draw back in June 1957.

And these mind-blowing figures are more than enough to be going on with for now. Because you're already mumbling to yourself, "If about 40% of Britons now hold Premium Bonds, that's like saying … every single person with brown eyes."

Never mind the numbers. Don't you want to know something just a little bit more basic?

WHAT ON EARTH ARE PREMIUM BONDS?

WHAT DO YOU KNOW?

When I started writing this book, the people at NS&I told me two things about Premium Bonds that have stuck with me all along:

Premium Bonds are a serious yet fun way of saving
Premium Bonds are the brand of Middle Britain

Rather than take this as read, I saw it as a challenge that I had to meet. There was something to prove. Serious. Fun. Saving. Middle Britain. Ideas were beginning to take shape.

And then I thought to myself, "What do I know about Premium Bonds?"

So, looking for some clues and inspiration, I went to Trafalgar Square, where Harold Macmillan launched Premium Bonds back in 1956. I found myself walking around the area,

HAROLD MACMILLAN LAUNCHES PREMIUM BONDS IN TRAFALGAR SQUARE ON 1ST NOVEMBER 1956

tripping over kerbstones, thinking about Premium Bonds … how the totality of numbers and bond holders and accumulated money are big and getting bigger … how London's meeting points and confluences, like Piccadilly Circus and Trafalgar Square, are small and getting smaller. I'm on the Strand. Used to work here. One or two theatres dotted around. There's the musical, *Chicago*. Saw it aeons ago. Still going. What keeps it alive? Is it an alternative to whatever London musical is fashionable? We-will-rock-you-mama-mia-our-house-life-is-a-cabaret-don't-cry-for-me-Argentina?

Chicago stays the same but changes. There's a clue here, somewhere. Tony Hadley, ex of Spandau Ballet, is the lead star of the moment. Hmmm … to cut a long story short, if you're under 35 or over 60, you may not have heard of him. The 35 to 60 age range – now, where has this been figuring in my thinking about Premium Bonds? Is it something to do with relevance? Yes, that's it. Relevance to a particular point in your past that's still important today.

The very next thing I did when I knew I was writing this book was to find out from my family, friends and business associates, most of whom are aged 35 to 60, exactly what they knew about Premium Bonds? Perhaps they could enlighten me. How relevant were Premium Bonds to their lives? More specifically, I asked 100 of them what came into their heads when they thought about Premium Bonds. And you know how it is, once you press a button, people don't hold back with their thoughts and opinions …

"… My granny. The 1960s. Black and white TV … Old people scrimping and saving and putting their money away for a rainy day – and then being disappointed that their cash has not amounted to that much … Security. Unadventurous. Risk averse … Teabags. £1 notes. Grannies … Legitimate gambling … One of the few envelopes from a financial services company that I like to see coming through the door. Always feels like you're getting something for nothing … Not savings, more of a 1970s lottery ticket … A more innocent time, my mum and dad's house, Radio 4, record players, the Archers, tinned ravioli … Tradition or the past and it's safe … You need to invest a big chunk, at least £2K to have a chance of winning … I'm sure Ernie or whatever the computer is called doesn't recognize the old style numbers I have. I wonder what £5 was worth in 1965 … Why would I want to support the Government anyway? I think they are a bunch of profligate leeches and add little or no real value to most people's lives … They were considered a safe gamble in my mother's time … I had some as a child, which were cashed to decorate my bedroom the way I wanted it when I was nine or 10 – we moved out of the house a year later … Old-fashioned, out-dated. Something our parents bought in the 70s/80s … Is this not just another way to boost government funds? It feels like they have been replaced by the National Lottery. Are you more likely to win something on the National Lottery?…I do consider the funds in Premium Bonds differently to my other monies. Psychologically it is different – they are 'extra to' my other savings. There is also a thrill about any winnings as opposed to appraising the interest earned on investments … Safe and traditional way to save with added bonus of the taxman not getting any of the benefits!…We have a friend who has invested 1,000s and wins something every other week. Perhaps she's just a lucky cow!…I get feelings of guilt because I know I've got some somewhere and should check to see if I've won anything but never get around to it … Something people my age used to be given as birthday presents by aunties. ERNIE … Old-fashioned. Football Pools. The man from the Pru door to door insurance era … Blimey, do they still

exist! My mother in law has some ... Financial investment package with no guaranteed return on investment. Monthly prize draw. You can buy a bond for £1 and it is run by the Government. You can get your pound back at any time ... It also makes me think of fun – the opportunity of winning without costing anything ... a never-ending lottery ticket ... The look of an official certificate, pastel paper, I think green, about the size of a large cheque. ERNIE. An association with other Bonds of the Premium Bond era – Brooke Bond, James Bond ... Hope mingled with anticipation and excitement! ... I do have a Premium Bond that was bought for me by my mother when I was a baby or boy. I keep it in my filing cabinet with my school reports and exam certificates ... I hive off a percentage in anticipation of paying income tax. So far it has worked out about the same or better than putting the money in a savings account. My accountant gave me the idea – great or what? ... A better bet than the lottery, at least you are not wasting your money and I want at least some chance of becoming a millionaire..."

PUT YOUR MONEY WHERE YOUR MOUTH IS

OK, that's it, I've got the message. The book's written. I may as well pack up and go home. Hang on a minute! Is that the sum total of all there is to know about Premium Bonds? But then, I'd only asked for a *feeling*. So, I probed a little deeper under the skin.

If you had a sudden windfall of £30,000 and didn't immediately need to do anything with the money, would you put it into Premium Bonds?

"I would probably buy some shares or put it in a more modern product like an ISA. My perception is that the return is not great and that I could do far more productive things with that amount of money – what I'm not entirely sure ... I'd be happier to take a greater risk and potentially receive a greater gain than putting it into bonds ... I'd buy an antique Fender Strat ... If I'd money to top up what I had, I would put it in as you don't tend to 'touch' it as much as money in your regular savings account … I wouldn't have thought of buying more Premium Bonds with my windfall. Is it a good savings scheme? I really don't know. More likely to cash it and get a loft extension … I'd probably put it in a high interest easy access account but I would consider Premium Bonds because they're safe, there's no gamble and there's always the chance of winning the big one … If I had spare cash I'd rather put it into something that can either guarantee a level of income or produce extraordinary gains at a risk … No way!!! Got to be better investment opportunities … Maybe – my father-in-law put a lot of his savings into Premium Bonds and makes a better return than average bank interest rates … I would pay the money towards my mortgage … The thing is I've had more fun out of them than my shares – there's no worry about losing money, only the opportunity to win it."

PREMIUM BONDS IN A DRAW SOMEWHERE

No interest! No inflation-proofing! Never you mind! Back in the fun days, no wonder they used Frankie Howerd to advertise the value of Premium Bonds. Titter ye not!

Everybody knows something about Premium Bonds. Of course, it's what they do about it that counts.

MEMOIRS OF A LAPSED PREMIUM BOND HOLDER

Simon Harrop, CEO of the Brand Sense Agency, says: "My view of Premium Bonds is entirely nostalgic. I don't really know what they are, how they work or who runs them. I think it's the Government but it all seems rather SMERSH-like.[1] Think I have about £10 worth of Premium Bonds given to me by an eccentric great aunt in 1965 on my first birthday. I seem to remember last seeing the certificates about seven years ago shortly after getting married, whilst moving to a new house. They were in a red plastic wallet about the size of a passport. I think they are in my 'memories' shoebox. This is an old Clarks Commandos box into which I have placed small keepsakes of nothing in particular, a Matchbox superfast Mini Cooper, an Action Man diving helmet, a letter from my first girlfriend (we were nine). I have never checked my numbers to see if I've won anything. I don't really know if you have to check up or if they (or Ernie?) come to find you. Anyway I wouldn't really want to check. Half of the appeal and mystery is knowing that the Premium Bonds are in the attic somewhere and maybe there are a million pounds or more in a London vault waiting for me to claim them. Finding out that after 41 years I have won nothing would be a huge disappointment! If I had to associate a smell with Premium Bonds, it would be musty old books – the smell of the attic. Taste? Arctic Roll – like strawberry jam rolled in cardboard with a dollop of vanilla ice cream spoilt by ice crystals. Lots of promise, disappointing delivery! Sight – a vision of my great Aunt's front parlour. The room that we were never allowed to play in as kids. Sound? 'The Wombling Song' or the creak of an attic door. Touch? Crinkly old paper or a heavy bar of gold bullion."

PREMIUM BONDS – THE REALITY CHECK

WHAT, EXACTLY, ARE PREMIUM BONDS?

It's only natural to keep asking that question. Because, despite all these feelings and perceptions, you still haven't got to the bottom of it. You need someone just to give it to you straight.

Premium Bonds are the flagship product of NS&I, a government-backed agency which exists to attract funds from you, individual savers in the UK, in order to fund what used to be called the Government's public sector borrowing requirement and is now called the Public Sector Net Cash Requirement (PSNCR). This is the money the Government needs to fund its activities over and above what it gets from public taxation. Basically, it's the budget deficit in the UK, the difference between government expenditure and government income. Well, you did ask!

PRO:	CON:
Safe, backed by the Treasury	The value of the Premium Bond is eroded by inflation
Anyone aged over 16 years can buy them	You do not receive any interest on your investment
Parents, grandparents, great grandparents or guardians can buy them for children under 16	You are not guaranteed to be a winner
You can invest up to £30,000	
The same Premium Bond can win again and again	
Bonds can be cashed in at any time	
Winnings are tax-free	

Bonds. Premium Bonds. The Government raises money by issuing bonds, which are secured loans. With Premium Bonds, the Government promises to buy back the bond for its original price on request. That's the "Bond" bit. Now, where does "Premium" come from? The Government pays interest on the Bond – not to every individual who buys one, but into a prize fund. From this prize fund comes tax-free prizes, or "premiums," to those lucky people whose numbers come up. There's more.

When they were first launched by Conservative Chancellor, Harold Macmillan, they were called Premium Savings Bonds. Although the Government today still considers Premium Bonds a form of saving, the "Savings" bit got dropped somewhere along the way.

For a national institution, Premium Bonds seem a bit of a "background" brand – a back-in-the-60s-and-70s brand. And, with all the interest-bearing, instant-access financial products on the market today, Premium Bonds shouldn't stand a chance. But their popularity has rocketed in the last five years, selling more than in the previous forty-five. And when they announce extra £1 million prizes,

THE FIRST PREMIUM BONDS JACKPOT WAS £1,000

sales go up astronomically, even though the chances of winning £1 million are, for most people, much lower than winning the National Lottery (one in 14 million). Then again, there are over one million other prizes per month.

But never mind the big numbers. What is the on-the-ground reality about Premium Bonds?

The minimum amount of Premium Bonds you can now buy is £100. The maximum amount you can buy is £30,000.

There are many ways to do it: online, via *www.nsandi.com*; by phone to NS&I; by post from NS&I; at your Post Office®.

The odds of winning a Premium Bond prize change over time:

February 1993	**11,000–1**
May 1997	**23,066–1**
June 2003	**30,000–1**
March 2007	**24,000–1**

Yes, but who picks the numbers? There are, after all, so many numbers. Now, that's where ERNIE comes in. ERNIE, I hear you ask? He's important enough to get a chapter all to himself. Yet, right now, he's a little bit vague in the memory?

JUST WHO IS ERNIE?

Who is ERNIE?

(a) The fastest milkman in the West.
(b) Eric's sidekick.
(c) A machine designed to control inflation and encourage thrift.
(d) I don't know, I'm under 40, can I go now?

Apparently, UK Conservative Party leader, David Cameron, picked "Ernie, The Fastest Milkman In the West," as one of his eight favourite records on *Desert Island Discs* in May 2006, claiming: "When you are asked to sing a song, this is, I'm afraid, the only song whose words I can remember." David William Donald Cameron turned 40 on 9th October 2006. Are Premium Bonds on his radar?

ERNIE – Electronic Random Number Indicator Equipment – is the machine at the very core of Premium Bonds, whose monthly job it is to produce all the winning numbers. A whole nation depends on him. NS&I wants to keep its two customers happy – you and the Government of the day. You want your numbers to come up. The Chancellor of the Exchequer wants to pay off the National Debt.

NUMBED BY THE NUMBERS IN THE NATIONAL DEBT

What is National Savings & Investments? I've heard it say that "NS&I are the people's savings and investments going into the National Debt." Oh, that! How do I grasp the significance of the National Debt, NS&I's role in paying some of it off and my own insignificant part in it? NS&I manages about £78 billion in savings, amounting to 10% of the UK savings market and accounting for 16% of the UK's National Debt. The National Debt is around 42% of the nation's GDP. According to the International Monetary Fund, the UK's GDP in 2005 was about £1,173,400,000,000. At 42% of this, the UK National Debt is £492,828,000,000. And, using this figure, 16% of the National Debt is £78 billion. So, there you have it. It all adds up. No shenanigans. And you know that your Premium Bonds are going towards the good of the country. Even though you know not where, you ought to be happy. Especially if you're getting a decent return.

IT'S NOT AS SIMPLE AS YOU THINK

From your little bunch of Premium Bonds to paying off American war loans in the National Debt, it's just too much to contemplate. So, the customer face of Premium Bonds is so simple. It helps if you have an inkling about what lies beneath, the mechanics of it all. But you don't really have to know. Maybe you don't really want to know.

At its simplest…

The odds of a £1 Premium Bond winning a prize depend on how many prizes are dispensed in any one month in relation to how many Premium Bonds are in the draw.

The amount of money available for prizes is called the Prize Fund. It is calculated by the Prize Fund Rate – the rate of interest which NS&I charges the Government for borrowing money from the British public via Premium Bonds.

The number of Premium Bond prizes available is calculated by a formula set by NS&I which currently states that 10% of the Prize Fund will represent prizes at the top level, £5,000 and over;

10% will represent prizes at the middle level, £500 to £1,000; and 80% will represent the lower level prizes, £50 and £100.

PREMIUM BOND WINNERS

VALUE AND NUMBER OF PRIZES AWARDED IN APRIL 2007

£1 million	2	£5,000	335
£100,000	17	£1,000	4,146
£50,000	33	£500	12,438
£25,000	67	£100	236,148
£10,000	167	£50	1,186,745

Prize value **Number of prizes**
£103,687,050 **1,440,098**

£1 MILLION WINNER NO. 1: A man living in the London Borough of Hounslow
Bond number: 121AC715181 – Bought in December 2006
Total holdings: £21,640

In the London Borough of Hounslow:
• nobody had ever won the Premium Bonds jackpot previously
• nearly 300,000 people own Premium Bonds worth over £110 million
• there are over 2,500 unclaimed prizes worth over £146,000.

£1 MILLION WINNER NO. 2: A man living in Aberdeen
Bond number: 049WF012332 – Bought in June 1998
Total holdings: £7,400

In Aberdeen:
• two people have won the Premium Bonds jackpot previously
• more than 63,000 people own Premium Bonds worth over £86 million
• there are over 2,000 unclaimed prizes worth over £130,000.

At this point, the more financially astute of you may have a mental picture of a dog chasing its tail. The odds of winning are dependent on the number of prizes; the number of prizes is dependent on the size of the Prize Fund, which itself is dependent upon the Prize Fund Rate. But the Prize Fund Rate itself isn't permanently fixed. What is it dependent upon? And aren't your personal odds of winning dependent on how many Premium Bonds *you* have in the draw?

Well, there's the little matter of the Bank of England Base Rate. And, as for your personal odds, I'm coming to those.

In the meantime, just how difficult all this is to grasp – unless you've got a calculator, a gallon of caffeine and a degree in maths – only goes to show how ingenious this brand called Premium Bonds really is and how financially incapable most of us are.

And, if you turn over a few stones, it only gets more complicated…

In March 2007, NS&I wanted the odds of winning a prize to remain at 24,000–1, as they had been for over two and a half years. It helps maintain public confidence in the fairness of the system. This meant that over 34 billion Premium Bonds were competing for over 1.4 million prizes (do the maths).

Not bad, when there are two £1 million prizes up for grabs.

But hang on! For every £1 Premium Bond you hold, you have a one in 24,000 chance of winning a prize. Ultimately, your odds of winning a prize depend on *how many* Premium Bonds you have in the draw against how many Bonds are in the draw in total.

If you have 30,000 Bonds in the draw, then you effectively have 30,000 "1-in-24,000" chances of winning a prize. Which means that, on average, you are odds-on (but not guaranteed) to win a prize that month and about 15 in an average year.

A prize, not necessarily *the* prize. Think about it – 80% of prize values are at the lower level of £50 and £100. Only two out of over 1.4 million prizes are the £1 million jackpots. Even for a 30,000 Bond holder, the odds are astronomical at over one in half a million. But definitely worth a shot. Especially so, when there are five £1 million pound prizes up for grabs, as there were in December 2006 and June 2007. And, unlike the National Lottery, you get to keep what you invested for the next draw.

But two people do win every month. On 1st June 2007, the 50th anniversary of the very first Premium Bonds draw created the 188th millionaire winner of the Premium Bonds jackpot since this prize was first introduced in 1994. In July 2004, an East London woman scooped the £1 million jackpot with a holding of just £17 bought back in 1959. Her odds of winning at the time were one in over 1.4 billion. Unlikely, but true.

IT'S A MYTHSTORY...

Q: Is there anything in the theory that people should sell and re-buy Premium Bonds every two or three years in order to stand a better chance of winning?

NICE LITTLE ERNIE: Just out of interest, I can only give you one good reason for doing this. If you feel you haven't been very lucky with your existing numbers, then cash them in and buy some new ones. Of course, if you do so, you'll miss out on the next monthly draw, because you have to have your Premium Bonds in my system a whole month before they become eligible. And that might just be the month you get lucky...

YOU CAN WORK IT OUT

While you try to get your head around the "nice" odds of one of your Bonds winning a Premium Bond prize, the other part of your brain is failing to compute just how impossible the odds are of ERNIE coming up with one of your numbers out of 35 billion. To do it, you would have to have a brain the size of a planet, like Marvin the Paranoid Android, and you'd probably be as depressed.

Me? I'm no expert. No degree in maths. I don't drink a lot of coffee. I own a calculator. That's about it. I'm here to analyze the brand and my brain is just about frazzled. Remember, it's the size of a small rock, just like yours.

It's actually much simpler to forget the big prizes and just concentrate on the return on your investment, if you're that way minded.

At the time of writing, the Prize Fund is 3.6% of the total current investment in Premium Bonds. As each prize is tax-free, this is equivalent to 6.00% for a higher rate taxpayer and 4.50% for a basic rate taxpayer. If you're winning prizes, that is.

You calculate how well you are doing on Premium Bonds in any one year by adding your end of year winnings to your beginning of year stake and dividing by that stake. If you started with £10,000 and won £360, the equation is $((10,360/10,000) - (1)) \times (100)$. Then make the adjustment for your lower or higher rate tax band. This will tell you how your money is faring against typical AER interest rates offered by other tax-free and tax-paying instant access savings accounts.

In March 2007, the best cash ISA currently pays 5.8% AER tax-free. So, as a lower rate tax payer your Premium Bonds return on investment would have been lower, at 4.5%. But still higher than inflation. As a higher rate taxpayer, you would have been quids in with your tax-free £360 worth £600 to you, £20 more than you could get from your tax-free ISA.

Strangely enough, at the time of writing, the best cash mini ISA happens to be NS&I's own Direct ISA. However, until April 2008, you can only invest £3,000 a year in cash mini ISAs, while you can hold up to £30,000 worth of Premium Bonds. So Premium Bonds remain very attractive for higher rate tax payers who also want to lodge larger sums of money. Set this against the best taxable savings accounts available in March 2007, offering between 5.25% and 5.65%, and you'd be even better off. Don't tell me Premium Bonds are not an investment!

WHO MANAGES PREMIUM BONDS?

Overall, the unique business model known as National Savings & Investments is run by just 130 people employed directly by NS&I and 1,700 outsourced to Siemens. The centre of the Premium Bonds world is Blackpool, home of most of the operational activities. Durham and Glasgow house NS&I call centres for telephone customers.

THE PARTNERSHIP WITH SIEMENS

In April 1999, Siemens Business Services (now known as Siemens IT Solutions and Services – SIS), became responsible for the day-to-day running of National Savings on a ten-year contract, with an option for five more years. When 4,153 staff moved from National Savings to Siemens, it was the biggest transfer of staff from the civil service to the private sector. The benefits to National Savings were immense. Running the service in-house for 15 years would have cost £793 million, whereas Siemens is running it for £635 million, being able to invest cash in transforming operations more quickly. The main benefits have been cost reduction, IT investment, modern systems, quicker market response, and dynamic customer service.

In Blackpool, besides Premium Bonds, they run a Tracing Service and administer Pensioners Guaranteed Income Bonds, Guaranteed Equity Bonds and Income Bonds. In Durham, it's ISAs, Savings Certificates and Fixed Rate Savings Bonds. In Glasgow – Easy Access Savings Account, Ordinary Account, Investment Account, Capital Bonds and Children's Bonus Bonds.

So, Premium Bonds are just one of the products offered by NS&I, a government agency. Some people just see politics in this. Most do not see anything at all.

NS&I Head of Marketing and Communications, Tim Mack: "In financial services customers never quite know who owns who. But our brand owes so much to the fact that the Treasury made us an Executive Agency and gave us considerable autonomy. As a result, Premium Bonds are not seen as political. And, technically, every citizen is our shareholder."

Do you see yourself as a "shareholder" of National Savings & Investments?

As Premium Bonds recover from the champagne celebrations of their 50th birthday, NS&I can, does and has to carry out a great deal of research to reassure itself and the Government that Premium Bonds are on the radar of a significant portion of the British general public. Being on the radar is one thing. It's what people think about Premium Bonds that counts. What do you think?

WHO MANAGES PREMIUM BONDS?

According to an Ipsos MORI poll carried out for NS&I in Winter 2006:

35% of all **adults** did not know who managed Premium Bonds
9% of all **NS&I customers** did not know who managed Premium Bonds

27% of all **adults** knew that NS&I managed Premium Bonds
68% of all **NS&I customers** knew that NS&I managed Premium Bonds

22% of all **adults** thought that the Post Office managed Premium Bonds
12% of all **NS&I customers** thought that the Post Office managed Premium Bonds

12% of all **adults** thought that the Government managed Premium Bonds
9% of all **NS&I customers** thought that the Government managed Premium Bonds

Sometimes, to explain statistics you need more statistics…

1 in 4 of the population had got the message that NS&I runs Premium Bonds
1 in 5 of the population still thought the Post Office runs Premium Bonds
1 in 10 of the population thought the Government did
2 in 3 NS&I customers knew that NS&I runs Premium Bonds
1 in 5 NS&I customers thought the Post Office or the Government did

But what do these statistics mean? If you were working in marketing communications at NS&I, where would you apply your thinking?

Now we know something about Premium Bonds, perhaps we can get back to the question we really want answering… "But this is *Premium Bonds* we're talking about here – so how come they're so successful?"

Mark Brooks, Head of Media and PR at NS&I: "What has changed is that they are marketed differently. From the 50s till the 80s, they were marketed as a fun way of saving and investing, in many ways a more sophisticated lottery. The more serious message of recent times has led to a wholly different perception of Premium Bonds, which has turned into a massive escalation in sales."

But again, there's more to it than that…

Is it the Post Office? Most of you still buy your Premium Bonds at a branch of the Post Office, the UK's largest retail network. The Post Office still accounts for 60% of all NS&I product sales. Premium Bonds still owe a great deal to the Post Office, which has run its own advertising and marketing campaigns in 14,000 branches in support of a product which is not its own…

Is it the marketplace? In 2006, NS&I Chairman, Paul Spencer, said that people were still not yet moving capital away from cash-based savings and investments like Premium Bonds and ISAs and towards stocks and shares…

Marketing. Marketplace. It's all of these and much much more…

None of this makes any sense without going in search of Middle Britain.

COME IN MIDDLE BRITAIN, YOUR NUMBER'S UP

WHO, WHAT, WHERE IS MIDDLE BRITAIN?

Personally, I think we'll get right into the heart of Premium Bond country if we find Middle Britain. But what, where or who is Middle Britain? And when?

How come I'm smiling to myself as I ask these questions? Is there something amusing about the phrase, "Middle Britain"?

When comedian, Chris Addison, produced his TV documentary, *The Hunt for Middle England*, [2] he could find very few people who would own up to being Middle England. Addison found himself hunting the elusive beast, as if riding to hounds (very un-Middle Britain).

Is it a location? Is it embodied in a certain type of person? Is it something that used to exist and is now but a lingering memory? Addison never once mentioned Premium Bonds. But then, very few people from Middle England would talk to him or reveal their true selves. Do we have to let our politicians decide for us where and what Middle Britain is?

MIDDLE BRITAIN: THE CHARACTER AT THE HEART OF PREMIUM BONDS

Middle Britain made Premium Bonds successful. Middle Britain sustains Premium Bonds today. Middle Britain doesn't like to identify itself. Anything else?

Middle Britain mustn't grumble, but complains a lot

Middle Britain pays its taxes but grinds its axes

Middle Britain will not stand up and be counted but insists on being heard

Middle Britain supports diffidence, not difference

Middle Britain rules the waves but does not waive the rules

Middle Britain is not Jade Goody, but it could be David Beckham

Middle Britain is not football, but it is cricket

Middle Britain rejects big change and donates small change

Middle Britain is not in my back yard, but possibly in yours

Middle Britain hates gambling, but likes a flutter

Middle Britain is neither a type of person nor a place on the map. It is a heartbeat, a pulse rate, that goes up and down with the years. And Middle Britain is a bundle of contradictions that's in all of us to a greater or lesser degree, as long as we're brave, polite, honest, diligent, tax-paying, compassionate, animal-loving, tolerant, suspicious of intellectuals and maybe foreigners, too.

MIDDLE BRITAIN: CONSERVATIVE WITH A SMALL C

Middle Britain: from Harold Macmillan to Tony Blair, via Harold Wilson and Margaret Thatcher, politicians have risen or fallen on their ability to track its pulse and keep with the beat. Just take a look back (and in the back of this book) at all the socio-economic and cultural history of the last 50 years.

In the colourless early 50s, despite the Coronation and Festival of Britain, it felt like the war was still on. The population was on rations until 1954. When Harold Macmillan launched Premium Bonds, it was in the middle of the Suez Crisis of 1956. People were sick of war. There was a huge desire for an optimistic future and successful politicians of the time rode the wave.

When Macmillan became Prime Minister in 1957, he told Middle Britain that they'd "never had it so good." People wanted to believe it. What they didn't want to believe was the second half of that quote, which ran, "What is beginning to worry some of us is, is it too good to be true?" Nobody wanted to overstretch themselves. For Middle Britain is nothing if not conservative with a small C.

Things ran smoothly until the 1970s. Edward Heath took Britain into Europe, a matter of national pride after several rejections, but his Conservative government suffered at the hands of industrial disputes, which held the country to ransom and virtually closed it down. When Labour got back in, matters only got worse. Industrial relations were in turmoil and inflation was rampant. A product like Premium Bonds does not operate very well in periods of economic turmoil and inflation.

Middle Britain was really suffering. Then came a whirlwind which personified everything Middle Britain thought it stood for – Margaret Thatcher. A resurgence of Middle British values against unions at home and assertive powers in Argentina and the European Community. But ten years is a long time in Middle Britain and, when there's nothing left to sort out, governments tend to meddle with the natural rights and standards that are dear to many. You can't tinker with Middle

Britain. Brought down by the Poll Tax she may have been, but it was really boom and bust economic mismanagement that did for Margaret Thatcher's government. And a product like Premium Bonds does not operate very well in roller coaster economic cycles in which recession features.

By the 90s, Middle Britain's pride was taking a real buffeting, as the culture was being shaped by the National Lottery. And, just when we thought Middle Britain was going to dive lemming-like over the millennial cliff – we've seen the resurgence of a brand that lies at the very heart of it – a national treasure that has grown beyond belief until it has become a brand fit for the 21st century.

NATIONAL TREASURES, HOW WE LOVE THEM!

Winston Churchill, Buckingham Palace, Florence Nightingale, Alton Towers...Alton Towers?! We've all been ducking and diving, chucking and jiving, trying to hang on to the tailcoats of everything our forefathers fought for – and it seems we've lost our sense of direction. We no longer know which way is up. That-was-the-week-that-was has transmogrified into Get-me-out-of-my-big-brother. In the meantime (and it's been a very mean time), we've moved from 'asbeens to asbos and the only bad thing we've managed to ditch is asbestos. Bum bum! There's a bit of Blackpool, for you! And Blackpool, having faded and now regenerating, is still with us. And Premium Bonds, growing in glory, are with us more than ever, if only you looked. Not exactly larger than life, but still the stuff Middle Britain puts aside for a rainier day.

YOU AND YOUR FOIBLES

Despite the success and continuing appeal of one of Middle Britain's favourite brands, there is a sense that Middle Britain lies lost and lonely, somewhere between the chavs and chavnots. There's such a warm feeling of security about them in times of great instability and uncertainty.

Premium Bonds have suffered their ups and downs, particularly in periods of inflation. But they're still here and stronger than ever in the hearts of Middle British people who represent the shrinking silent majority, the solid backbone of the country, the basic and consistent ingredient in an ever-changing national recipe.

The basic flavours of Middle Britain seem to be tolerance, reticence, stability, continuity and a general ability to laugh at itself. The Middle British way of looking at the world is quiet, decent, long-suffering, keeping itself to itself, passive until roused, the foil to bullies of all kinds. Its foibles are reflected in all our great comedy programmes.

ONLY WHEN I LAUGH

The British state of mind that both created and sustains a brand like Premium Bonds may be lurking somewhere between…

Life with the Lyons and *The Catherine Tate Show*
The Goon Show and *The Young Ones*
Hancock's Half Hour and *Only Fools and Horses*
The Clitheroe Kid and *Auf Wiedersehen, Pet*
The Dick Emery Show and *I'm Alan Partridge.*
The Likely Lads and *To The Manor Born*
Steptoe and Son and *The Vicar of Dibley*
Dad's Army and *Men Behaving Badly*
Monty Python and *Vic Reeves' Big Night Out*
It Ain't Half Hot Mum and *Yes Minister*
Fawlty Towers and *Little Britain*
Rising Damp and *Tittybangbang*
Last of the Summer Wine and *Absolutely Fabulous*
The Good Life and *The Royle Family*
Keeping Up Appearances and *The Office*

And if you can't find your Middle British self in all of that, there are plenty more in the timeline at the end of this book.

It's all there. But what is it, what isn't it? Middle Britain is just a snapshot of the people of this country at any one time, as far away from the edges and extremes as it's possible to get. It's nowhere and everywhere, everything and nothing. I'm in it. You're in it somewhere. No wonder I'm smiling when I think of Middle Britain!

THAT'S THE TICKET

Ever since we became used to the idea that everything is relative, meaning that nothing is secure or any longer as it was or should be, our social values have become brand values. But some things never change: politicians, British sporting prowess, Premium Bonds.

Personally, Premium Bonds remind me of Liquorice Allsorts. And now I see they're rebranding the Bassett's confectionery range. Better hadn't ditch Bertie!

Premium Bonds also remind me of Wallace & Gromit. Or should that be the other way round? They're a modern British product representing old British values. They make you smile, raise a certain wistfulness for something long forgotten, but not quite lost forever. It's a spirit that can be recaptured. That's the ticket!

While I'm trying to remember what Sir Alan Sugar said last year, I find myself wondering why they never made a film called *Carry on Saving* back in the 50s or 60s. You can imagine Kenneth Williams uttering, "Can I make a withdrawal?!" And Barbara Windsor tittering, "But you've got to make a deposit first!"

If you look around, you can see other brands that embody this British spirit. Sir Richard Branson's Virgin empire is a brand that takes this spirit from defending the little man against the establishment, as so many Ealing Comedies did in the 40s and 50s, to pushing the boundaries of exploration, as Scott of the Antarctic did, as Harry Potter does.

On the one hand, there's the intrepid, never-say-die nature. On the other, there's the funfair for the common man. Gluing them together is this honesty, integrity and fairness. It's not the sentimental American hand-on-heart kind of justice. It's not the

33

shoulder-shrugging French sort of superior equality. It's quiet, understated, determined, beneath the surface. And above all, it's just fun. It's British.

LOOK AT IT YOUR WAY

FEVER PITCH

Here's my Bond Fever Pitch. If Britishness is going to be taught in schools, then Premium Bonds ought to be on the curriculum. The essay question might be something like this: "Comically conservative, quietly optimistic – consider this description of the British social character in the light of the success of Premium Bonds over 50 years."

Of course, I've been answering that question myself. I really just want to know what Premium Bonds mean to people.

People seem to like Premium Bonds because they don't really see them as a brand, in the sense that almost the entire world that surrounds them is branded to high heaven.

Despite the Sir Alan Sugar connection (or maybe because of it), Premium Bonds show very little interest in coming out as a brand. Premium Bonds do not appear to be part of this world of showy, exhibitionistic OTT-statement. Bonds are the light hidden beneath the invisible bushel at the end of the dark condition known as British, or rather English, understatement (and that was my attempt to get into Pseud's Corner). This may very well be clashing with the burgeoning sell-your-granny-on-eBay-you-are-what-you-excrete-get-a-boobjob culture – which, for upcoming generations is normal and acceptable.

FUTURE MEMORIES

In this culture, the hand-me-down nature of Premium Bonds may meet some immovable obstacles. In my nearest Morrisons supermarket the other day, I came across a few shelves marked "Polish." Far from Mr Sheen and other smelly surface shiners, what I discovered was a small shrine to the arrival in our midst of a significant Eastern European community. Odd-shaped bottles and cans with unintelligible labels described a culture whose focus seemed to be…pickled gherkins. The knowledge of Premium Bonds tends to remain within families, getting passed down by word of mouth. As our society gets more diverse, and we welcome people from Eastern Europe and other parts of the world, who is going to tell *them* about a culture that includes Premium Bonds?

Hot off the press is the possibility that Britain could become the first European nation to issue bonds that comply with Islamic law.[3] There's nothing like a commercial imperative to inspire brands to address markets previously thought unattainable. Although several Muslim countries, including Dubai, Malaysia, Qatar and Singapore, issue some of their national debt in Islamic bonds, Sharia law forbids the payment of interest. Besides which, gambling runs contrary to strict Islamic tradition. Now that mainstream banks are tapping the commercial prospects of this market (Lloyds TSB recently announced it would offer Islamic business accounts as well as current accounts), however, NS&I will need to adapt its products accordingly. Premium Bonds are among the first NS&I products to be tested for suitability. It's a big marketplace.

So, the ability of Premium Bonds to carry memories into the future with current generations will be interesting to observe. You don't suddenly fall in love with the brand just because you reach 40! But, believe it or not, every generation holds something sacred. Personally, I hope that I will never wake up to headlines that Premium Bonds are being re-sold on eBay – one of the few things in life that aren't.

BUYING AND SELLING

For NS&I, the simple truth is that people buy and people sell Premium Bonds. In truth, it's far from simple – I guess this relationship between Premium Bond sales and repayments is one that the organization needs to monitor very closely.

Although sales and repayments can both go up in the same month, NS&I has to note the percentage of Premium Bond repayments against sales, as it can provide a barometer of the good times and bad times. In good times, repayments are around 33% of sales (although in the strong sales period of 2006/7, repayments were around 50%). In bad, it can clearly go over 100%, into deficit. When the figure goes above 66%, the people at NS&I start to twitch and look for reasons. At such times, all they have to ask themselves is, "Is it us or is it the economy?"

THE SALES AND REPAYMENTS BAROMETER

As well as being a good barometer for the way the trend is going, the repayment against sales percentage tells some interesting social stories. In the early days, sales would always increase year on year, but there would be periods in which many people simply got fed up and cashed them in. In 1966, perhaps people just needed the money to buy tickets for England World Cup matches. In 1975, the repayment figure reached 58%, but inflation was 26% and the Prize Fund Rate was only 5.5%. People had not experienced inflation like this before. During the patriotic Silver Jubilee fever of 1977, sales took their biggest leap since launch. Then, people were more ignorant than now about the value of an investment. In 1990, 9 out of 12 deficit months were a real sign that Britain was slipping into recession.

IT'S YOUR PERCEPTION

If they're going to get into the heads of upcoming generations in an ever-changing Britain, however, Premium Bonds will have to be very proactive. Over the past few years, it's been tough enough for the good people at NS&I to convert media commentators and opinion formers. Despite Premium Bonds being the flagship product behind National Savings' role in reducing the National Debt, back in 1998, a writer in *Revolution Online* magazine could say that he thought the presence of Premium Bonds on the recently revamped National Savings website was "slightly out of place." because Premium Bonds were "that great pre-Camelot government-sanctioned flutter."[4]

While very few media commentators could possibly make that mistake in 2007, following all the TV advertising and marketing drive, too many still gloss over Premium Bonds and pay scant attention to other NS&I products. Their authors tend to be financial experts who just don't seem to recognize the combined economic, social and cultural investment that people make in Premium Bonds.

Even defender of the people, the Consumers' Association, better known as Which?, barely recognizes the rocketing public interest of recent years: "A popular gift for children are NS&I Premium Bonds. Strictly speaking, these are not investments, although if the holding is big enough and the child has average luck, the 'return' can compare easily with middle-of-the-road bank and building society rates and, of course, there's always that outside chance of making a million." [5]

Is this view any different from that of the general public? People just aren't as passive these days. And the sales figures of the last five years suggest something entirely different is going on.

Are Premium Bonds really about saving? Are they about gambling? Or are they purely about winning? You will keep asking!

Notes

1   SMERSH (СМЕРть Шпионам, meaning "Death to Spies") was a counterintelligence department in the Stalinist Soviet Union founded just before World War II.

2   *The Hunt for Middle England*, shown on BBC 4 on 4th March 2007.

3   Greg Hurst and Robert Cole, "Ernie could be taught to obey strict Islamic law," *The Times*, 23rd April 2007.

4   "National Savings," *Revolution Online*, 14 October 1998.

5   Jonquil Lowe, *Be your own Financial Adviser*, (Which? Books, 2005).

2

CARRY ON DREAMING
THE CULTURE THAT PRODUCED AND SUSTAINS PREMIUM BONDS

YOUR MONEY
OR YOUR LIFE

IT'S BIGGER THAN YOU

Premium Bonds are part of a culture called Britishness. Within this culture co-exist a myriad subcultures – rugby club, Women's Institute, snooker, online networking, DJ culture, Middle Britain, there are just so many. Whichever subcultures we belong to, we often look with bemusement at the way other people exist alongside us in worlds which seem so different to our own. Yet, before we reach up to our universal Britishness, there are things we have in common at lower levels. Our interests may divide us, but some things unite us all.

Take money, for instance. We all need money. And there are many ways to get it. One way of making sure you have some of it in the future is to spend less of it in the present. At the lower level we call it Saving. At the higher end, it's Investing. Another way of getting it is to take a risk and put what you could be saving into a bet on the near future. It's called Gambling. In current British culture, which doesn't really know whether it wants to be understated or over the top, the best way to look after the future is to enter competitions and put your dreams up for grabs. It's called Winning. And you can win big, so big that it becomes a dangerous question of your money or your life.

Saving/Investing. Gambling/Winning. Whatever, it's the money subculture and we're all in it.

RESISTANCE IS FUTILE

Although we live in a world of super-casinos and lotteries today, historically, British society has shied clear of overtly encouraging gambling and winning, in favour of promoting the idea of thrift and personal responsibility for the future. But, there is something in the British soul that likes to fight doing stuff for our own good. Unless, of course, there's an irresistible incentive.

FROM WILLIAM GLADSTONE TO GORDON BROWN

The UK government recognized the need to raise money outside the normal method of direct taxation around the middle of the 19th century, when Chancellor William Gladstone established National Savings in 1861 as the Post Office Savings Bank. The case was presented as a means of allowing workers to save as well as providing the Government with resources to service its debts. A Poor Law reformer of the time described it as so thoroughly good a measure, he wondered how it ever passed. To this day, many people still associate Premium Bonds with the Post Office – which is not surprising, as the Post Office Savings Bank launched Premium Bonds in 1956 and the Post Office still sells billions of Premium Bonds for what is now National Savings & Investments. However, in 1969, National Savings split from The Post Office to become a nationalized government department under the Treasury. In 1996, National Savings became an Executive Agency of the Treasury, one of more than 100 Executive Agencies of the UK government, free to manage the implementation of policy. In 1999, National Savings operations were outsourced to Siemens. Renaming itself as National Savings & Investments in 2002, NS&I now has a bigger job to do for the Government than ever and much of the work is done by Premium Bonds. Between 2003 and 2008, NS&I was tasked with raising £15 billion net. It achieved it a year early.

Yet when Chancellor of the Exchequer, Harold Macmillan, introduced the idea of Premium Savings Bonds in his annual budget of April 1956, insisting they would bring in "those members of the community who are not attracted by the reward of interest, but do respond to the incentive of fortune,"[1] there was general laughter in the House of Commons.

Labour spokesman, Harold Wilson, called Premium Bonds "a squalid raffle...a national demoralization." He wanted Macmillan to take Premium Bonds out of his proposals and allow MPs to examine the idea in more detail as part of the Government's bill on gambling and betting.

Lord Mackintosh of Halifax, chairman of the National Savings Committee, and with hindsight, a lot wiser than

laughing MPs of the day, said he hoped that Premium Bonds, with their tax-free prizes, would attract "millions of people who had so far not found the conventional forms of savings attractive."[2] Mackintosh belonged to a Methodist church that opposed Premium Bonds. He was quoted as saying, "If we can't save sinners, at least we can make sinners save."[3]

MUSTN'T LAUGH

People have always laughed at Premium Bonds. Try it with your friends. Ask if they've got any and watch their reactions. It's probably a nervousness about talking money.

In our British culture, we don't like talking about money. It seems ... well, foolish to do so. Governments, on the other hand, have to talk about money. They hold lots of it and it belongs to us. Back in the 50s, governments were eager to give some of it back – for your own good.

Were you there in the 1950s? People who were have told me the 50s were dull. The war was not over. Not the kind of war that we know – terrorist explosions, distant cities, things that happen to other people – but something that involved every fibre of everyone's being and consumed them for years after VE and VJ day.

When Premium Bonds entered into this world of deprivation, they were a brilliant, innovative, if controversial product. People were talking about Premium Bonds then in the way they're talking about super-casinos now. Harold Macmillan hit a moment in time.

Premium Bonds were launched with the advertising line, "Saving with a thrill." Try saying it in the voice of Harry Enfield's Cholmondeley-Warner character and you might just get it.

Today, we smile when we see the word "thrill," largely because we tend to use it in an ironical sense and are unable to see it in its original form. In the 1950s, people did not have this complexity. Life was post-war, not post-modern. Although rationing had ended by 1954, it was revived again in late 1956 due to the Suez Crisis, just as the Government was promoting Premium Bonds as a way of saving for a better future. Whatever, back then, people were more than eager for a thrill. Most weren't yet used to Elvis. Austerity still had the nation in its clutches. There was nothing to spend and less than that to spend it on. Thrill, yes! Save? Surely not.

IS THE BIG FLUTTER A BIG FLOP?

This was the question asked by the *Daily Mirror* on 16 February 1957, months before the first Premium Bonds draw had even taken place. Although £48 million of sales occurred in the first month, November 1956, only £7 million occurred in the second, December. In January 1957, this was even lower. The chairman of National Savings, Lord Mackintosh, who'd run the Wings For Victory campaign during the war, had predicted £150 million by the end of March 1957. But he still considered it a success, saying that Premium Bonds had brought in nearly £60 million in three months, more than the Football Pools companies take in a year. The *Mirror's* conclusion belied its headline: "There is some evidence to show that one big objective is being achieved in some areas. Instead of reducing other forms of national saving, the bonds are tapping the pockets of those who have never saved before."

CARRY ON SAVING

WHAT MAKES US SAVE?

The purpose of Premium Bonds was to help control inflation and to encourage more people in the post-war period to produce a higher level of savings. Premium Bonds were a new, non-risk approach to persuade those who had the money to save but chose not to.

The academic definition of savings tends to be the act of postponing consumption, or disposable income minus consumption. There are other irritating terms such as the average propensity to save (APS) – the proportion of disposable income that is saved rather than spent, also known as the Household Savings Ratio. Of course, we all know instinctively that future growth is made possible by forgoing present consumption to increase investment!

Yet, in a fast-moving consumer-focused economy, don't people prefer to spend rather than save?

The Department of Work and Pensions seems to think that, overall, people in the UK are more predisposed to spending than saving. It seems we prioritize current living standards over saving for retirement, even though we are living longer in retirement. [4]

OR RATHER, WHAT STOPS US SAVING?

Market research tells us that levels of saving are falling in the UK. The Mintel Report on UK consumer attitudes to saving [5] even uncovers some serious psychological inhibitors preventing people saving. Would you believe that consumers feel the main deterrent to saving is "a lack of money"? No joke.

Government has to take this kind of thing seriously. Over the past 20 years, they have made you take a much greater responsibility for your own financial wellbeing. Trouble is, the modern obesity trend notwithstanding, you've got healthier and live longer, putting an even greater strain on your hopes of a better future life. You've had little choice but to start taking greater control of your financial situation and think about putting money aside for your old age. But, what do you go and do? Blow it all on a series of games ranging from bingo to the National Lottery.

THIS NATION'S SAVING DISGRACE

It's the economy, stupid! Why save when you can get credit so easily and the world just wants you to have more? OK, more than six in ten adults are saving towards something, three in ten are saving through a pension and almost half are saving for non-

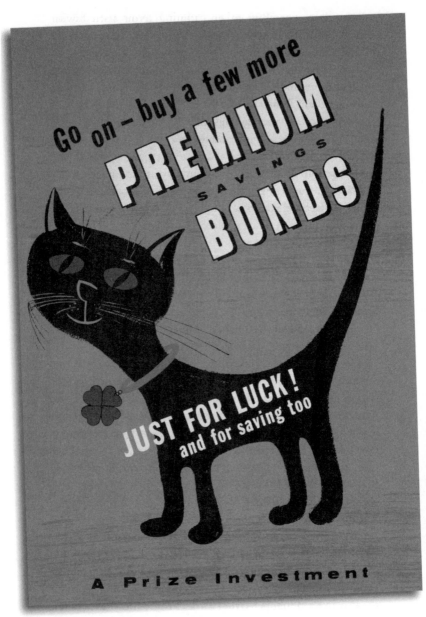

AN EARLY PREMIUM BONDS POSTER

retirement reasons. But go on, admit it, you started with relatively small amounts each month and now you're putting even less aside, aren't you?

Although UK households have amassed financial assets totalling more than £3 billion, 16 million of you are currently not saving anything at all. Where is it all? Who has it? Are you minding the "savings gap" – the shortfall in what you need for your old age and what you are actually saving towards it?

Twelve million people are currently at risk of under-saving. Your appetite for saving is diametrically opposed to your appetite for gambling (and eating!). But you've had other reasons. Too many products, too much choice, too little understanding.

When it comes to saving, higher earners will try to take advice from independent advisors. But you know there's no such thing as a free hunch. Meanwhile lower earners, it seems, would rather listen to their children. Are your kids more clued up than you are?

There's a general lack of trust in financial services providers, influenced by so many stories of so many people being mis-sold an untold number of times. Or, as Mintel puts it, "43% of adults in Britain clearly state that they do not trust financial companies. More than four in ten consumers would rather invest in property than savings products." Yet somehow, in a world of mistrust, people do put their faith in Premium Bonds and National Savings & Investments.

KIDS DO IT...DADS DO IT...
EVEN ANTIQUATED CHAVS DO IT...

But not young adults.

According to Saving for Children (which describes itself as "the only independent website dedicated to saving for your children's future"), "Children have a positive attitude towards saving, with nearly half setting aside some money each week." [6]

If so, what happens to this attitude when they reach adulthood? Apparently, half of British teenagers are in debt by the time they are 17 and the UK is becoming a nation where adults are increasingly having to support their children through their adulthood. Research by GE Life shows that 64% of parents provide their adult children with financial assistance and continue to do so when their children have their own offspring.[7]

You're least likely to save between the ages of 15 and 24 and the most likely to get into debt. Your propensity for saving money appears to peak between 45 and 64. Much of the debate on saving centres on planning for retirement, which is why it is such a turn-off to young people. This must translate to other savings products. If you're in your 20s and 30s, Premium Bonds may well be more alien to you than any other generation.

However, Premium Bond alienation is not confined to the current generation of 20- and 30-somethings. Those who are in their 40s and 50s today felt much the same when they were younger. It seems that grappling with the concerns of adulthood makes everyone quite forget those little bits of paper called Premium Bonds gifted by granny when they were small. Intangible, untouchable, unrealizable, they had little significance back then and even less now that you are in the high-spending 20s and 30s, focused on borrowing, not saving.

Don't worry, it will all come back to you. It's just what happens with Premium Bonds.

CARRY ON GAMBLING

ARE PREMIUM BONDS SAVINGS OR INVESTMENTS?

People are confused. Not least because the terms "savings" and "investment" are used interchangeably. To help establish whether an asset is saving(s) or an investment you should ask yourself, "Where is my money invested?" If the answer is cash then it is savings. If it is a type of asset which can fluctuate in nominal value then it is investment. Any the wiser?

Financial author, Jonathan Reuvid, describes Premium Bonds as a form of "passive saving." "Once you have chosen where to put your money, you don't need to do anything more until you come to draw the cash. Unless, of course, you find somewhere better to put it and decide to switch." The last sentence seems to contradict the idea of "passive." And, considering that around 40% of you own Premium Bonds – remember, that's 23.6 million of you owning £35 billion – then Premium Bonds are a brand that has surely put the massive in passive![8]

PREMIUM BONDAGE

My brother-in-law, Pete, has a background in accountancy and finance and seems to spend his whole working life dealing with risk and attitudes to risk. Pete has coined a phrase which has a special meaning in the context of this book – Premium Bondage. "Why Premium Bondage? Because after you have held them a few years the face value of the original investment has been eroded so much in real terms it hurts to cash them in and realize the loss. So you leave them tied up with National Savings."

Other detractors of Premium Bonds say most bond holders are paying something for nothing – a negligible return on a decreasing stake. There are some people who refuse to mention Premium Bonds in the same sentence as savings and investments.

Online discussions argue interminably over whether Premium Bonds have the right to be called an investment. People get quite agitated about it, insisting it's just a flutter with a difference. You stand a chance of winning and you can get your original stake back at any time. And some of these people refuse even to use the word "stake" in regard to Premium Bonds at all, because the money invested is not inflation-proof.

What does someone think who has never won a penny from Premium Bonds in 37 years? In 1969, Paddy Dewey invested £100, liking the idea of the monthly jackpot. Now retired, Paddy said: "'My investment was a lot of money at the time, it was nearly one month's salary for me, so I was expecting it to be a good investment."[9] So, it was an investment when she put the money in, and a gamble 37 years later when she'd won nothing!

Had Paddy invested her £100 in equities in 1969, it would have been worth £843 in late 2006. If she'd put it in a building society, it would have been worth £153. NS&I said that with average luck Paddy should have won at least three £50 prizes and, with her £100 holding, that would be worth £250. The £100 still gives her a one in 169 million chance of winning one of the two £1 million jackpots.

IT'S A MYTHSTORY...

Q: Is it true that Premium Bonds are neither a saving nor an investment, but a gamble of the interest you could otherwise earn in top interest-bearing accounts?

NICE LITTLE ERNIE: Just out of interest, I never hide the possibility of winning nothing or eroding capital. And I don't take a chance with the truth. Even though I'm hidden inside a room inside a place very few people ever visit, I want to be transparent. In everything I do, I want to show that I'm on the side of British customers.

ARE PREMIUM BONDS A GAMBLE?

As far as NS&I is concerned, the thinking is clear. Press Office spokesman, Jonathan Akerman, said: "The over-riding message from when they were launched is 'savings with a thrill.' In recent years, with the launch of the National Lottery, there was a fear of some contamination, that people would regard Premium Bonds as a gamble, as a chance to win mega-bucks. So we have re-emphasized that Premium Bonds are still a savings product, designed to encourage people to save." [10]

GAMBLING WITH THE VALUES OF MIDDLE BRITAIN

The biggest gamble with Premium Bonds could be for a government which plays with the standards of Middle Britain. In 2006, around the time when the Government was pushing through a new bill of its own on gambling, the Home Office issued NS&I with guidelines allowing prisoners to buy Premium Bonds for the first time, having just banned National Lottery ticket sales to prisoners, on the grounds that the former was an investment and the latter a gamble! [11] In 2004, imprisoned rapist, Iorworth Hoare, won £7m on the Lotto Extra after buying a ticket while on weekend leave from Leyhill open prison. In March 2007, lottery millionaire, David Dyas, was found guilty of serious sex offences against two schoolgirls committed several years before he won several million pounds in 1998. [12] It's all bad publicity for the National Lottery. Normally, Premium Bonds benefit from this. So, is it a mistake to shut the door after the horse has bolted for the Lottery, then open it for Premium Bonds, a brand with deep integrity? Let's hope that NS&I never has to take a £1m cheque into Strangeways or Pentonville.

How about financial advisers? "We wouldn't say 'don't do it,'" said Justin Modray from Best Invest. "They are a safer way of having a flutter."[13] "Premium Bonds are worthwhile for just about everybody," said Garry Spencer of Wilbury Financial Management "You are guaranteed to get your money back. It's a no-lose situation; it's really like having money on deposit. With the Lottery, you are just throwing your money away. It is a tax on the vulnerable. People get into a rut with it and, in a sense, they are addicted. It is a dream for them but, realistically, it is never going to happen."[14]

People will make those comparisons, but Diane Thompson, Chief Executive of Camelot, doesn't entirely agree: "It is entirely misleading to compare the National Lottery with Premium Bonds ... The lottery is not an investment product, nor has it ever been marketed as such. It is a harmless flutter that has raised more than £19bn for good causes. It has also made millionaires of more than 1,900 of our players, as well as creating around four million winners every week. Incidentally, the odds of winning a prize with a £1 Lotto ticket are just one in 54, compared with one in 24,000 on Premium Bonds."[15] In which unwitting comparison, the last bit of information is itself misleading, as the lowest Lottery prize is £10 and the lowest Premium Bonds prize is £50. And you can always get your money back.

THE EVILS OF THE LOTTERY

MPs listened to evidence of forgeries and fraud, of a worker left penniless by her foreman because of his addiction, of a woman who robbed her father of his hard-earned savings to pay for her habit, of mothers who neglected their children, of men who became gamblers and turned to drunkenness and idleness. These social evils were all attributed to the lottery. 2006? No, 1806. Encouraged by the scourge of slavery, William Wilberforce, The Committee of the House of Commons was set up in 1808 to see how the evils attending lotteries could be remedied by law. In 1826, State lotteries were outlawed and not seen until 1994. You know the rest.

It's the way you put it. Journalist, Neasa MacErlean, wrote, "If you are making a cold-headed evaluation [of Premium Bonds] you should consider the possible returns."[16] This implies that if you're making a hot-headed decision, ah, what the hell...

Attitudes have changed over the years. In 1973, the Page Report into National Savings thought that "the public seem to regard the Premium Bond with a degree of good natured scepticism...from the investor's point of view, Premium Bonds are not 'good saving' or even a particularly good bet."[17] It concluded that people who bought Premium Bonds were technically "saving," but noted that they took care not to buy too many Bonds and actually went to other forms of saving to which they were very definitely "attracted by the reward of interest."

In our world of relativity, our "investments" and "gambles" have to be seen in comparison with other investments and gambles. At which point it becomes clear that Premium Bonds are both.

CHANCE WOULD BE A FINE THING

Of course, there's gambling and there's gambling. Journalists of both the left and the right have damned the UK Government's fast-tracking of new gambling legislation onto the statute books. As a form of gambling, Premium Bonds have to exist in a media world where very strong opinions have been voiced. Take the Government's determination to support the creation of a super-casino, first awarded to Manchester by an independent committee, then quashed as an idea altogether by a narrow defeat in the House of Lords. To condense a myriad media views...

...there is no popular demand for more casinos ... it's only the gambling industry that stands to gain millions ... it's like the easing of the licensing laws and will only lead to the very opposite – binge gambling ... the only victims will be the poor, tempted to part with what little cash they have in the forlorn hope of escaping with a million ... far from representing the best interests of their constituents, local authorities only have eyes for the revenue opportunities of casinos on their doorsteps ... nationally, it's just another stealth tax to support public borrowing ... we already have a National Lottery to fleece the poor ... even Premium Bonds have two £1 million prizes on offer now ... we still have Football Pools, Bingo and Bookies ... and, to cap it all, we now have online betting...it's a wonder anyone still owns their own house, the shirt on their back ... gambling isn't the only growth industry – what about the bailiffs?

Sod 'em! And Gomorrha! To hell with tomorrow! We live in a culture which is making it easier for people to gamble today. There can be no squabbling over that statement.

NO TO THIS GET RICH QUICK SCHEME

I'm not talking here about the rejection of the Government's plans for a super-casino in 2007, but the rejection of the introduction of Premium Bonds during the First World War back in 1916. Robert Kindersley, Chairman of the National War Savings Committee, objected to Premium Bonds as part of the war effort in "The Ethical Case Against Premium Bonds." He called the idea a lottery because the holder would be giving up part of their interest for a chance of winning a prize. And that such an appeal was not to higher things such as patriotism, provision for old age or sickness, self-denial for the sake of the Forces. Oh no, Premium Bonds appealed to baser human instincts, to the idea of get rich quick and to a weakness of human nature – the very negation of the spirit of steady and persistent individual effort needed at the time. Kindersley's view prevailed and the idea was dropped. He campaigned against it whenever it was raised later. He died in 1954, two years before Macmillan re-introduced the idea. Even then, Macmillan inserted "Savings" in between Premium and Bonds to offset any criticism that this was a lottery.

HAVE THE LAST WORD

What do you think? The last word on gambling should always be with the British public. In January 2007, the BBC news website published its readers' views on their experiences of buying Premium Bonds.[18] Some talked about saving, some about winning. In the true spirit of British feedback forums, most talked about fair play, i.e. they complained. The answers they published ought to be engraved on the heart of every marketer and creative agency associated with Premium Bonds.

"The view that Premium Bonds favour the rich is idiotic! If you buy 1,000 lottery tickets you clearly have more chance of winning than if you buy one ticket. Don't you understand maths or statistics?"

"More prizes at the lower levels would make bonds an attractive prospect."

"Premium Bonds used to be for the small saver... but now you cannot buy less than £100 and the less well off cannot do that."

"I agree that the newer numbers seem to win. I recently changed all of my small amounts into one large block and have had several wins."

"If you've got less than £100 to invest, and you're looking for a sure-fire return in the short or even medium term, then don't invest in Premium Bonds. But if you fancy a chance of winning £1,000,000 while retaining your original investment, it's the only game in town."

"Holding £100 of Premium Bonds is like buying two lottery tickets a week for a year and then being able to use them in every draw for as long as you like before selling them – pretty good compared to the lottery."

"Had many bonds for 40 years, not a single win. Waste of time for decent working people."

A 1970s PREMIUM BONDS POSTER

"The mistake people are making here is to regard Premium Bonds as an investment. They are not, they are a form of gambling, and if you don't win, you lose the interest you would otherwise have earned. Simple! People should stop complaining and if they're not happy, invest in or gamble on something else."

"The whole point of Premium Bonds is to encourage people to save. The more you save, the more bonds you have and the more chance you have of winning something. What part of that do people have difficulty understanding?"

All very revealing about the British character but…savings, investment, gambling…are you any clearer? Oh, the British love affairs with hope, glory and maths. You have to smile, don't you? Just as you have to be in it to win it. But I believe that's someone else's line.

CARRY ON WINNING

HUMAN EMOTION

If Premium Bonds are neither saving nor gambling, maybe they're part of something bigger – something that many financial analysts and media commentators have simply missed out of their number crunching. I'm talking about the human element in all of this – the *emotional* investment in a brand they see as different to anything else on the market.

But it's surely all about winning, isn't it? We all want something for nothing, don't we? None of us wants the super-casino in our back garden, but we'd all like to meet Agent Million. The Premium Bonds people have been informing the jackpot winners in person since they raised the top prize to £250,000 in 1980. For many years, there were the people who delivered the prizes. Then, in 2003, there was Agent Million.

We all like to win. Winning is everything. Much of what we do and what we see is tied up with "winning" – bargains, freebies, anything as long as it's something for nothing.

What is this "winning" culture all about? What does it say about us? Are we really moving towards an American view of money? Are we trying to escape our culture and identity or hang on to it?

When it comes down to it, the prospect of winning is your idea of saving.

To win, or not to win, that is the question.

IT'S A MYTHSTORY...

Q: Is it true that you have to have the full £30,000 in to stand a chance of winning anything?

NICE LITTLE ERNIE: Just out of interest, this is the biggest complaint I get from the public, particularly when I'm doing local radio. Before they've even passed the time of day, it's "the 30K or nothing" accusation. But people need to think of it as a raffle. The more you buy, the more chance you have of winning. If one Premium Bond has about a one in 17 billion chance of winning the monthly jackpot, then a holding of 30,000 has about a one in 567,000 chance of winning.

Just as there is an undercurrent in British society which says that "money goes to money," there is a perception that only people with the largest holdings win Premium Bond prizes.

But perceptions of unfairness do not stop the less well off majority being attracted by the lure of the million pound prize. When NS&I announced that there would be five millionaire winners in the December 2006 draw to celebrate the 50th anniversary of the launch of Premium Bonds, 2.2 billion were sold in October alone.

WHAT'S YOUR GAME?

Bingo? Football Pools? National Lottery? TV quiz shows? Premium Bonds?

According to one enterprising journalist, "Winning is not a matter of luck, it's about shortening the odds."[19]

Come on down, sir! Yes, you, the smiling gentleman in the Hawaiian shirt with the receding forehead. Some of us know that if you look the part and fit the profile, you can get on those TV quiz shows that offer big prizes. It's a question of getting clued up. If you want to get on *Who Wants to be a Millionaire?*, you need persistence and the ability to pay a phone bill of up to £1,000. But if you look out for new TV quiz shows, which are desperate for contestants, you may get invited to turn up for an audition. Make sure you overstate your clothing and understate your intelligence. They're looking for bright personalities, rather than big brains.

---

88 – TWO TRADITIONALLY BUILT LADIES!!

Three million of you play bingo regularly. A night out at one of the UK's 688 licensed clubs only costs between £15 and £20. Five hundred of these clubs link up to the national bingo game, twice a day every day, except Christmas Day. It offers the biggest prizes and is the country's second largest computer-controlled game after the National Lottery. The top prizes increase through the week – from £50,000 on Monday and Tuesday, £100,000 on Wednesday through Saturday and £200,000 on Sundays. Not forgetting 15 regional prizes of up to £5,000 and individual club prizes. What's the lure? Well, apart from the social club aspect, a £10 stake gives you a 200,000–1 chance of a win on the national game – far better odds than most other big prize games and lotteries. Play bingo on Friday 13th because the odds are better – that's the day when thousands of superstitious bingo players stay at home, and your odds of winning the national £100,000 prize could be anything around 30,000-1. My mother-in-law goes every Friday night and never wins. Unfortunately, all her friends do. She accepts her below-average luck, "I go for a good night out. I couldn't even win the skin off a rice pudding!"

And how can we forget the National Lottery? More than four million of you win every week on the draws and scratchcards. Weekly players tend to spend £3 a head. It can be quite lethal online. Once you've put some credit in, you can feel the urge welling up inside you to play one of those dozen or so scratchcard games just one more time. But then, you're trying to get your mind around the fact that the National Lottery has

A WINNING MENTALITY

Adam is a 30 year-old Environment Manager working for a top FTSE 100 company in Reading. He owns a two bedroom apartment and has £9,750 in Premium Bonds.

"I bought the first £5k in a batch, and then dribs and drabs over the past year. Last time I checked the bonds, I was over the average return. There is one £1,000 bond batch which seems to win more often – the last two wins have been about five single unit digits away from each other.

"I enter competitions when I see a prize I like the look of! Generally, I seem to win. I have an 80% strike rate. Entering and winning is great fun and very rewarding. Am I lucky? Hard to say. One makes their own luck in life.

"My winnings? Here's a quick run down from memory: £500 or so in Premium Bonds over the past year; £1,000 limited edition mountain bike; VIP passes to Silverstone; numerous concert tickets – Ordinary Boys, Southport Dance Weekender, Queen and Abba tribute bands, Massive Attack; organic hampers; £1,000 cash – radio breakfast show; £750 electricity and gas vouchers; £560 radio "beat the clock"; £450 radio prize tickets to cinemas, theatres and concerts; £200 Debenhams vouchers; £100 HMV vouchers; £100 Specsavers vouchers (I don't even wear glasses); eight Eurostar tickets; stacks of CDs; iPod Nano; Christmas hamper; two trips to La Manga; four Stella Artois Tickets; £250 JD Wetherspoon drinks vouchers (to be spent in one night!); one meal for ten; one meal for four; one five-course meal for four on New Year's Eve, with private entertainment, and overnight stay in hotel; three meals for two; a large wide screen TV, DVD and VCR package and stand.

"Probably lots of other things, but I do not enter much, so the strike rate is very high!"

created over 2,000 millionaires since 1994. Including biggest ever winner, Iris Jefferies, who won £20,100,472 in July 2004.

Camelot has set the odds to make the whole thing as attractive as possible while bringing in the maximum yield. Although you only have a one in 14 million chance of hitting the jackpot, you do stand a one in 54 chance of winning at least £10. It's a curious fact that, despite the odds being way up in the millions, one in four of these jackpots is won by a syndicate.

There are those who insist that you stand a far better chance on the National Lottery if you pick numbers higher than 31, because there are no birthdays or anniversaries higher than that. But your regular numbers don't feature strings of consecutive numbers, do they? Your reasoning being that they never come up but one day they will? Well, many people think like you, so when they do come up and win the jackpot, you'll be sharing it with 10,000 others.

DOWN TO EARTH

After all this razzle-dazzle adrenaline junkie addictive behaviour, where does the rather flat, humdrum world of Premium Bonds come in? Well, isn't that exactly the point? Aren't Premium Bonds the simple, harmless alternative to all this glittering stress and debt-ridden hangover?

Many people continue to see the world in fixed terms – if the Government extends pub licensing hours, it may ease the last orders rush, but it's going to increase binge drinking; if it opens a raft of new casinos, debt and addiction will increase. There is a clash of cultures, of old values with new ways of behaving.

Within this constantly changing struggle for values, a spectrum with greed at one end and fear at the other, Premium Bonds continue to sit in the stable middle ground of the savings and investment market. Whichever way the economy swings, your money stays in and you have the chance to win a return on your investment. You're not forced into a choice between red and black or odd and even on a gaming table. You are investing in stability against a world of increasing relativity, choice and complexity. But always with the hope of winning the big prize...

THE THOUGHT OF NOT WINNING IS KILLING ME

Oh, the winning thing and how it bends people's minds! You've seen the anguish on the faces of people on Noel Edmonds' *Deal Or No Deal.* They've entered the show with nothing and are now worried to public tears (and this is in Britain) that they will miss out on the big £130K and leave with a paltry £40K. Remember the woman who said she couldn't go home to her family if she didn't accept the £13K, when she knew she could potentially win £57K?

Is there something here about losing a sense of reality? After all, to win anything is to lose the state of mind you had before you won it – that sense of hope, anticipation, that beautiful dream.

Now you've won the Lottery, you're pissed off because 17 other people won it with you. Instead of the £4.7 million you could have had, you've picked up barely more than £275K! What a bummer!

You woke up that morning with nothing (actually, that's not correct – you still had your beautiful dreams, worth so much when it comes to coping with the world). Now, all you have is £275,000, a shattered dream and complete uncertainty as to how you are going to handle your new world. There's the pressure from people, the stress of it all. Will you do a disappearing act?

To win is actually to lose. How many people can deal with that?

Nobody ever thinks about this. Yes, they talk about the evils of gambling, that debt-creating over-commitment to the pursuit of the dream. Perhaps we should pay more attention to the *evils of winning.* There are easier ways to create dreams than the pursuit of money. But once a money dream is shattered, there could be a lifetime of picking up the pieces.

And the point here is that, for many people, Premium Bonds are a cautious form of saving with a few nice surprises attached. It is nice to get that £50 cheque every now and again. And, if you never get one, it's nice to think that you might. It's not going to change your life. But it would be a nice little earner.

> **WOULD IT CHANGE YOUR WAY OF LIFE?**
>
> One elderly couple who had hit the £250,000 Premium Bonds jackpot in the 80s arrived in Blackpool carrying an empty holdall. They were persuaded it would be safer in the form of a cheque. It was suggested they take a taxi into town, but they thought it too extravagant. A senior member of staff escorted them to the nearest bus-stop and was solemnly offered 10p for his trouble.

AIN'T THAT PECULIAR?

Is this "winning" thing peculiarly British? The gambling habit in Asian countries is well-known. And many countries now have state lotteries, some paying out far more than any one person could possibly use. In America, where they dole out prison sentences that last lifetimes, they give lottery prizes that would last even longer. In March 2007, two American lottery ticket holders shared $390 million (£202 million). Or should I say three? There is another big winner – the US government will receive one-third of the jackpot in taxes – $130m.[20]

We're a very tolerant culture. We don't mind foreigners winning our money and helping us to pay off our National Debt. You do not have to be a UK resident to invest in Premium Bonds. Anyone over 16 can invest as long as their country of residence allows it.

Some countries do not allow their residents to win at Premium Bonds. The USA, for example, whose postal lottery laws forbid it. Hmm…it would be a bit like having US citizens contributing to paying off the UK national debt, much of which was owed to the US in the first place. And the Irish Republic, where the Gaming and Lottery Act ensures that Irish people contribute to the country's own lottery. There's nothing wrong with a little bit of protectionism, I say.

Of course, some people can go too far. An edition of *The Post Office Magazine* from 1957 tells a story of "a certain oriental gentleman who wished to register bonds, not only in his own name, but also in the name of his deceased ancestors and favourite patron saints."[21]

When Premium Bonds were introduced in 1956 Sweden had run irregular state lotteries since 1896, most recently in 1955 to raise funds for the State Opera. Finland and Greece had also had similar schemes.[22] The French had a bond where most of the interest was paid direct to the depositor with a small portion kept back in a "lottery" pool. But, although all were forms of money raising, the 1973 Page Report into National Savings considered none of them as savings.[23] In Britain, however, the only other chance of winning a large sum of money at the time was through the football pools. Interestingly, the Football Pools did not fall under any gambling legislation, because they claimed to be competitions of skill rather than chance! Ironically, they faded dramatically with the introduction of the National Lottery.

It's hard to imagine the Americans having anything like Premium Bonds. The fact that similar institutions to NS&I exist in countries highly influenced by the British – Canada, New Zealand, Ireland – surely says a lot. Yes, other countries have tried to follow in our eccentric footsteps.

NS&I Head of Marketing and Communications, Tim Mack: "Canada based its appeal on patriotism and families, but we've recognized that our ongoing appeal as a brand could not be based on heritage or patriotism. It has to be something else. It doesn't mean we have to have the best rates – although our Direct ISA is top of the charts. It's about sharing our brand values."

ALL IN A GOOD CAUSE

Everyone makes repeated comparisons between Premium Bonds and the National Lottery. They're everywhere. You simply can't avoid them.

In the end, however, any useful comparison between Premium Bonds and other forms of gambling becomes a discussion about values. About what people stand for and will not stand for. The public recognizes the potential danger of addiction and pays off its concern through lotteries and institutions that carry a "good cause" message.

We are individually responsible for our own personal attitudes towards gambling, but, for the institutions of gambling themselves, there is a collective accountability. Accountability is one of the biggest differences between Premium Bonds and the National Lottery.

When John Major introduced the National Lottery, he pointed out to detractors that our taxes were for the NHS, whereas the good causes of the National Lottery Fund were about people making choices. The perennial problem being that, people disagree about what "good causes" are.

Premium Bonds, however, have avoided this problem. On the one hand there is no confusion between gambling and good causes. On the other, people see Premium Bonds by and large as a good way of saving. Whether many wonder whether their money is going towards important aspects of the public sector is a moot point.

When he was Chief Executive of NS&I in 2005, Alan Cook said: "'The whole purpose of the organization is to raise money for the Government, and the whole value of our proposition is that we're backed by government. If we were floated and became a private company, we would lose our main point of differentiation."[24]

There is therefore the sense that governments need Premium Bonds more than ever, but that the brand is somehow beyond them, in that it pre-dated them and will post-date them.

Various governments have wondered about getting rid of Premium Bonds altogether but, to put it quite simply, there are just too many doors to knock down. There is an apocryphal story – meaning true but unattributable – about John Major describing how Margaret Thatcher had wanted to close the whole National Savings operation down. But Major pointed out how people saw it as saving for a rainy day. And how, when her government crashed the economy, that rainy day fund saved its bacon.

As the person responsible for Public Relations at NS&I, Mark Brooks knows that accountability is a question that raises its head and has to be answered. "Our people have to appear before the Treasury Select Committee. We're governed by the Freedom of Information Act. We've had to follow the EU money laundering regulations. We're members of the Financial Ombudsman Service, which deals with compliance. We've signed up to the Banking Code. OK, we don't publish how much we pay the Post Office or the financial elements of our arrangements with third party distributors. But we are transparent."

IT'S A MYTHSTORY...

Q: Just how can Premium Bonds account for themselves to the British public?

NICE LITTLE ERNIE: Just out of interest, look at me. I'm a Government agency with a huge income-generating capacity...for my size. I'm no bigger than a DVD player, for heaven's sake! OK, I'm not regulated by the Financial Services Authority. But listen, I am accountable to the Economic Secretary to the Treasury.

A MILLION OVER HERE IS NOT THE SAME MILLION OVER THERE

If public perceptions around accountability are what set Premium Bonds and the National Lottery apart, there's something else that marks a difference far more fundamental and identifies a significant pointer for the continuity of British culture.

Let me run this one past you like this. I'm beginning to think that £1 million won through the National Lottery would be an entirely different form of currency to £1 million won through Premium Bonds.

Why? This from the NS&I website: "Unlike winners of the National Lottery, Premium Bonds winners tend to keep their good fortune quiet. Their winnings are usually used to clear a mortgage or pay for a more comfortable retirement, rather than blow it on expensive purchases."[25]

Is this comment purely about the publicity aspect of winning a prize? Is there more to it?

SPOT THE DIFFERENCE

If you push them a bit further, value judgements about the differences between the National Lottery and Premium Bonds could conjure up a mental picture of two very different types of people. It may or not be true, but it's fun…

Maybe a National Lottery-type person might say…

"What's wrong with Aya Napa?"
"Got any fags?"
"I'm not recycling nothing…"
"Take that gold necklace off the cat!"
"Where's Stoke?"

Whereas a Premium Bonds-type person might say…

"Wouldn't that be a lovely surprise?"
"Fings ain't wot they used to be."
"Mustn't grumble, must we?"
"Is it time to take the dog for a walk?"
"I do like to be beside the seaside."

ESCAPE ROUTE OR REALITY CHEQUE?

We can take this fundamental point of difference a little further. As sure as our city streets are paved with chewing gum, our British thoughts are lined with golden dreams of leaving this very culture that we champion against allcomers. Sixty million people want to escape. Or do they?

Would you like to win a million? And your reason is?

Such questions as these are usually put to beauty contestants, enabling them to trot out carefully orchestrated answers. But, whatever we think of our own outer skin, we might just ask ourselves these very same questions. The answers we find are likely to be very illuminating about our character and the way we see the culture in which we live.

WOULD IT CHANGE YOUR WAY OF LIFE?

An elderly lady who had won £250,000 asked if her Premium Bonds prize could be just £10,000 instead. "I don't really want a quarter of a million. I just wouldn't know what to do with it."

Do you want to escape? Get away from all your worries, job, family, friends, culture, country? Would you throw everything away for this chance to assume a new identity? For that is what you would effectively be doing.

Or do you want to create a better position for yourself in your current way of life? Would you use the money wisely to help you live more comfortably and happily in your existing world? Far from escaping, you'd actually be hoping to confirm yourself in the culture.

Within this discussion is perhaps a clue as to the real nature of Premium Bonds and why sales have taken off since the launch of the National Lottery, when so many people predicted the opposite.

The National Lottery has that sense of glitzy escapism written all over it, in purple. You pays your money and you takes your chance. It's a crystal clear in-it-to-win-it mentality. An escape route to another life.

With Premium Bonds, you want to win. There's no doubt about that. But, if you don't win, you're in it next time. And there's a mindset about making adaptations to your current lifestyle, rather than throwing the whole thing away. Generally speaking, and no matter how much they criticize it and are encouraged by the media to do so, people love this country and realise how much it has to offer. For them, it would be a huge wrench to leave and set up anywhere else. And you know that, through a loan to the Government, you're continuously contributing somehow, somewhere, by reducing the cost to the taxpayer of funding the National Debt. A big Premium Bonds win is still life-changing, but it's more of a reality cheque for this life.

WHAT ARE THEY LIKE?

What's it like to win big on the Premium Bonds? When Hannah Peterson (name changed) won the £1 million jackpot in August 2004, it was her first win. Her winning Bond came from a £3,000 investment made in February 2003. When Agent Million knocked on her door on a moonlit night, Hannah thought she was going mad or that something had gone wrong with her Premium Bonds. Living on a pension of £108 a week, it changed her life. She bought a house as well as the maximum amount of Premium Bonds. She still gets a lot of pleasure out of those regular little wins.

When live-in caretaker, Graham Webster (name changed), won £50,000 in August 2000, he'd had Premium Bonds for 15 years and been buying them from time to time in blocks of £100. He agreed with his family to spend the money on a property which he can live in if he ever leaves his job. The Building Society manager gave him a funny look when he said he could buy the property outright, as Graham did not look like the sort of person who had a lot of money. He plans to buy more Premium Bonds as he believes his luck will never run out.

IT'S MUCH MORE THAN A KNOCK ON YOUR DOOR

If you've ever had that £1 million reality cheque from Premium Bonds, then you'll have received a personal visit from Agent Million.

If you personally are never going to win a million, do you think the next best thing might be knocking on people's doors and telling them they just have? (In a 2003 TNS Phonebus poll, only 2% of respondents said Agent Million would be their ideal job.) But I'm asking you to use your imagination here. Agent Million doesn't have to use her imagination. She does this every month. What is it like?

WOULD IT CHANGE YOUR WAY OF LIFE?

An elderly Lancashire man living in modest circumstances would not let the visiting officers in because he thought they were salesmen. On hearing that his wife had won a £250,000 prize, he said: "It won't make any difference to her. She'll still want to stay in this old house."

When I met Agent Million, I learned that there have been many life-changing stories, but one thing's for sure: "It isn't just a knock on the door."

The top secret nature of her identity and work prevents Agent Million from being specific about the winners she meets. Owing to the legally enshrined privacy surrounding Premium Bonds winners, I was unable to go on assignment with her to gauge the reactions of her latest £1 million winners in Birmingham and the West Midlands.

"I usually call around at 7.30 in the evening," said Agent Million. "With the soaps in full swing, you can be sure to find most people in at that time." But on dark, wintry evenings, with rain lashing the windscreen and the sat nav on the blink, it isn't easy touring the streets of our lowering cities in search of the right address, never mind worrying about whether she can catch someone in the break between *Emmerdale* and *Eastenders*.

Sometimes it requires the powers that only Agent Million can wield. On this occasion, she became he. And when he had located the first address, he made his way to the door. Knock, knock. Nothing. Knock, knock. Nothing. Not a curse, yelp, or bump to be heard. Nothing for it but to come back later. Have you tried finding a B&B in a dark Midlands city at short notice with a broken sat nav? All's well that ends well. Next morning, at 6.30, Agent Million is back at the winner's door, which now opens to reveal a lady readying herself for work. After a bit of yo-yoing back and forth and a few ID checks, he's helping the lucky lady to come to terms with the beginning of the rest of her life. You see, it never is just about knocking on the door and popping a cheque in the post.

As I debriefed Agent Million in a scrambled telephone conversation, I could just hear the relief in his voice. Another couple of millions delivered. And then back to Blackpool, where he became she once more.

AGENTS MILLION ON THEIR WAY

OK, you've worked it out now. There's more than one Agent Million. Sometimes it's a she (M1), sometimes a he (M2). Whatever, there's quite a little bit of investigative work to do before Agent Million can make that knock on the door. S/he can't arrive in a limo with a bottle of champagne in hand. What's the district going to be like? Is it best to arrive with a brief case or a carrier bag? Agent Million has to be prepared for anything. Sometimes, people want to call the police. At other times, they need first aid. And, yes, one suspicious wife marched her husband to the front door to confront the woman who had insisted on speaking to him without telling her the reason. Did she forgive him when she found out he was a millionaire? Who knows?

> **WOULD IT CHANGE YOUR WAY OF LIFE?**
>
> A "gentleman of the road" won £100,000. When he was encouraged to visit his local bank to open an account, he asked the bank manager to lend him £100 "to be going on with" until his prize money came through.

YOU SHOULD BE SO LUCKY

A WINNING PROPOSITION

Just why do people keep buying Premium Bonds in the numbers they do?

We must be a nation of gamblers. It's the dream of winning a big prize. The excitement generated by the brown envelopes that arrive telling you you've won any prize, however small. Isn't this what NS&I describes as the "fun factor"?

A VERY EARLY PREMIUM BONDS POSTER

Premium Bonds. Understated, loved but not talked about, very definitely not the National Lottery. All about saving and winning and making a contribution. Apart from the occasional little brown envelope with a small cheque, they are the recurring but unlikely idea of becoming a millionaire every month. People are waiting for that knock on the door.

IT'S A MYTHSTORY...

Q: Is it true that you have to buy in batches or blocks to stand a chance of winning?

NICE LITTLE ERNIE: Just out of interest, nowadays, you have to buy in a block of £100 anyway. This gives you 100 different chances of winning one of the two monthly £1 million jackpot prizes. As I've got a head for figures, I'd say that your chances of winning the jackpot were currently one in around 170 million. When they buy Premium Bonds, many people buy more than £100 worth. So, if they buy £5,000, they automatically have a block of 5,000 Premium Bonds. But the odds on any one Premium Bond in this block winning are exactly the same as if they had 5,000 separate Premium Bonds sprinkled throughout the system. By the way, if you think that consecutive Premium Bond numbers have a greater probability of winning, then you must think that a Lottery ticket with the numbers 44, 45, 46, 47, 48 and 49 has a greater probability of winning than, say, any other combination. It's just luck, my friend.

IN THE END, IT'S JUST A MATTER OF LUCK

Conspiracy theorists abound in the world of pot luck. Even the money websites are looking for patterns. The brands themselves build the myths. "That's the 134th time number 49 has appeared and the first this year." Oh no, not the 134th?! And I missed it! To me, this has always made about as much sense as if the announcer had said, "That's the three thousand and fiftieth sausage I've eaten in my life and the first since last Saturday."

Despite the randomness of the Premium Bonds draw, however, analysis of the winning statistics over a year inevitably throws up certain towns, names and signs of the zodiac that have been luckier than others. In 2006, the luckiest part of the country was the City of London where Bond holders won more £1,000+ prizes per million Bonds held than anywhere else in the country. In 2005, Oldham. In 2004, Sunderland. In 2003, Dumfries. At the time of writing, it's Glasgow.

Did you fare well as a Sagittarian in 2006? Taurus in 2005? Aquarius in 2004? Cancer in 2003? Consecutive Water, Air, Earth and Fire, eh? Even the elemental share-out is fair with Premium Bonds. The name Hannah also seems to be luckier than any other. It was the luckiest name in 2006 and 2004. In 2005, the luckiest name was Matthew, the only time a boy's name has entered the top spot.

Luck is important in life. When Napoleon was selecting his generals and names were brought before him, one of the first questions he would ask was, "Is he lucky?" Are you?

If you've won big on the Premium Bonds, you are lucky and in more senses than one. It's a dream come true. But it's not a dream of escape, absconding, life-rejection. It's a dream of acceptance, confirmation, affirmation. It's your money and it's still your life. And you can carry on dreaming.

Notes

1 *Hansard*, 17th April 1956, Vol. 551.

2 "1956: Macmillan unveils Premium Bond scheme," bbc.co.uk, 18th April 2006.

3 Jack Armitage, *Ernie, Son of Colossus*, manuscript in the NS&I archive.

4 Victoria Mayhew, *Pensions 2002: Public attitudes to pensions and saving for retirement*, Research Summary for the Department of Work and Pensions.

5 *Consumer Attitudes to Saving* – UK, Mintel Report, February 2005.

6 "Children have positive attitude to saving," savingforhildren.co.uk, 11th December 2006.

7 "Parents support children through adulthood," savingforchildren.co.uk, 14th February, 2007.

8 Jonathan Reuvid, *Where To Put Your Money*, Kogan Page, 2005.

9 Michael Clarke, "Britain's unluckiest Bonds holder," thisismoney.co.uk, 26th October 2006.

10 Neasa MacErlean and Jim Griffin, "Good old Ernie knocks out a thrifty fifty," *Guardian*, 28th October 2006.

11 "Prisoner Premium Bond ban lifted," bbc.co.uk, 13th February 2006.

12 "Lotto winner guilty of child rape," bbc.co.uk, 5th March 2007.

13 Neasa MacErlean, "Many happy returns?" Guardian Unlimited, 27th October 2006.

14 Neasa MacErlean, "Smart people are steering clear of the losers' lottery," *Observer*, 29th October 2006.

15 "Your letters," *Observer*, 5th November 2006.

16 Neasa MacErlean, op. cit.

17 *The Page Committee to Review National Savings Report*, HMSO, June 1973.

18 "Your Say: Premium Bonds," bbc.co.uk, 5th January 2007.

19 Jill Papworth, "Lucky break? Don't leave it to chance," *Guardian*, 27th January, 2007.

20 "Two share $390m US lottery prize," bbc.co.uk, 8th March 2007.

21 "£1,000 for £1, or The importance of being ERNIE," *The Post Office Magazine*, 1957.

22 "1956: Macmillan unveils Premium Bond scheme," op. cit.

23 *The Page Committee to Review National Savings Report*, op. cit.

24 Nick Mathiason, "The man who saved Premium Bonds," *Observer*, 14th August 2005.

25 www.nsandi.com.

3

JOURNEY
TO ERNIE
IN SEARCH OF A
MACHINE WITH
A HUMAN TOUCH

ILLUMINATING BLACKPOOL

MEETING THE PEOPLE AT NS&I

I just had to meet ERNIE. But first things first. There would be many more people to talk to before I could shake hands with the personality at the centre of it all.

The first time I visited the London headquarters of National Savings & Investments on the fifth floor of an imposing civil service edifice on Kensington High Street, however, I was flabbergasted that so much money could be generated by so few people. I met Mark Brooks, Head of Media and PR; Sue Simpson, Head of Brand; Tim Mack, Head of Marketing and Communications; Sally Swait, Premium Bond Manager; and Vicky Heron of Customer Insight.

Ever since National Savings operations were outsourced in 1999, there have been barely more than 130 people on a payroll responsible for collecting monies that represent 16% of the UK National Debt. Sue Simpson: "There is a sense of scale here. We talk in billions. Yet so few people are involved."

They tell me the atmosphere up in Blackpool is very different. That's where all the activity happens around Premium Bonds. To tell the truth, it always has done. I've read all about it, seen the pictures. Back in the late 1950s, the scene at Blackpool may well have been something like the film *Brazil*, starring Michael Palin – an intensively staffed world of filing systems, piled paper and clanking metal machinery. I had to see for myself. And, of course, Blackpool is where ERNIE lives. And, like I said, I just had to meet ERNIE.

DAYTRIP TO BLACKPOOL

In Blackpool, everyone knows someone who works on the Premium Bonds. "There is a pride around Premium Bonds here in Blackpool," says Nigel Laing, Operations Delivery Manager for SIS, or Siemens IT Solutions and Services. The bulk of the

500 staff at Blackpool are employed by Siemens.

As an outlet for sales, the Post Office gives Premium Bonds and other NS&I products a lot of support. A very different kind of support comes from Siemens, the commercial organization which has run NS&I's operations since 1999 and excelled on a number of fronts.

What bugs you most about the way financial institutions operate? They take a long time to get back to you? And when they do, the information is not always correct? In 2005/06, Siemens achieved 99.32% on timeliness, over and above its already high 97% target. And 99.29% on accuracy, against a target of 98.5%. Beat that (add your own bank's name here).

Talk to people in Blackpool, however, and there is very little mention of the company that took over the operation in 1999. And that's hardly surprising. Whether it's the call centre or the back office, people here are National Savings people – mostly long-servers, in their 40s and 50s who will always see themselves as part of the brand that brought our country Premium Bonds.

CALL ME ON THE TELEPHONE

In the Customer Information Centre, I am astonished at the difference in atmosphere between the top floor staff on the payroll and those on the ground floor from employment agencies. Upstairs, where people have been settled into the job for years, there's a relaxed feeling of business as usual. Downstairs, with a younger crowd, I meet a vibrant hubbub amid an array of 20-something hair-dos and low-slung jeans.

Team Leader, Lesley Scott, is proud of the contributions made by both teams. They co-exist in perfect harmony. Lesley presides over one of the newer buildings on the Blackpool site, in which the corporate colour scheme leans mainly towards NS&I, featuring some of the brand icons that first appeared about five years ago, with a new corporate identity around the changed name of National Savings & Investments – rows of unframed blocks of simple, straightforward beauty: a log round, orange slice, the conker.

Lesley's been here 27 years and that's about par for the course. I can't help thinking what happens when everyone reaches the age of 60. It's hard to imagine the call centre closing down. Although Blackpool remains the centre of the Premium Bonds world, there are other call centres in Glasgow and Durham, which share the load when amazing peaks occur, as they did in October 2006, in the rush to get signed up for eligibility for the 50th anniversary draw, with its five £1 million pound prizes. At such times, back office staff are called in from other buildings and it's all hands to the pump.

Lesley Scott talks about staff being very understanding of the peaks and troughs of demand and what is required at certain times. Through its "Just Ask" programme, NS&I is trying to encourage call centre staff to do more than respond to enquiries – a policy which seems to be working. Its key objective is to create a proactive customer relationship ethos. If staff have relevant, informed conversations with customers, levels of satisfaction will go up. How do you measure such things? Quite simple, really. Levels of satisfaction lead to higher sales. The Just Ask programme is achieving additional sales of £1 million per call centre team. 80% of the team achieved 99% customer satisfaction scores. Just the sort of thing ERNIE would expect.

AN ALTERNATIVE CENSUS

Back in the gigantic 70s concrete eggbox of the main building, Nigel Laing gives me a tour of the back office operations with all the detailed ease of someone who's been thoroughly immersed in everything to do with Premium Bonds for 35 years.

As he takes me through the building's many floors and departments, I get a sense of machinery and paper co-existing harmoniously in an office environment like no other I've experienced. Here, machinery aids the labour intensive nature of the work. With the records of 23 million Premium Bond holders held in many different ways – microfiched, taped, scanned, photocopied, filed, you name it – it is like an alternative population census, except it's far more efficient.

A machine will open envelopes on three sides and present it to an analyst, who determines which of 12 cages it goes into. They call it an information cleaning system. Everything is stripped of its content, analyzed, dealt with and filed in a way that you just do not associate with the inefficiencies and poor customer service of so many technologically driven businesses in the 21st century. People, paper and machinery have to work together here. And why should you be surprised that, besides ERNIE, there's a whole phalanx of machinery in Blackpool called ERIC (Electronic Remittance Imaging Centre). But, this time, he's not the funny one. ERIC simply takes the customer's application form and cheque, compares one to the other and sends both on their different ways.

Don't get me wrong. The office environment is similar to anything you'll encounter elsewhere. It's the numbers that are different. It's the way the organization adapts to the surging flow of information, which pulses in fits and bursts and isn't always predictable. OK, the Premium Bond buying habit tends towards the end of any one month and they average 220,000 items of post every month in the despatch room. But in October 2006, this leapt to 450,000. And this business, like any other, has key performance indicators it has to hit. All cheques received before one in the afternoon must be banked the same day.

In that amazing month that heralded PB50, or the 50th anniversary of the launch of Premium Bonds, they once handled about 17,000 cheques for £48 million in one day. The record achieved in that month was £2.2 billion worth of sales. When Nigel was showing a team from a third party distributor the ropes of the operation, they didn't believe him. "Surely you mean 2.2 *million*, was the response?" No, I mean *billion*!

GO TO WORK ON A LIFECYCLE

Once you get your head around this, you discover a new found respect for the people dealing so calmly with such numbers. And you understand a bit more why they're so into life-cycles

– anything that can affect the ebb and flow of applications and repayments.

There's one particular second when you manage to gather in your head the enormity of this operation for the lives of millions of people in this country, virtually on a cradle to grave basis. And then you lose it again. So you refocus on one particular cycle. There are about 22,000 death claims per month. This figure is very steady, but it is affected by extreme cold and hot spells. And who knows, maybe other human cycles – the housing market, City bonuses, England football performances, Tim Henman's Wimbledon fortunes, head office PR initiatives?! They're monitoring them all in Blackpool.

In this way, Premium Bonds are a kind of litmus test for our lives. They respond to the lifecycles around us. As Nigel Laing says, "Premium Bonds are a natural phenomenon about life and death. The dead are easy to deal with. The problem people are those who are still alive." And this thought lies at the heart of the work that NS&I does. It's trying to work out the lifecycles of customers from childhood to dotage, so that it can supply appropriate products at any particular stage. Except that, within this, Premium Bonds are the product with a difference. They're here for everyone, throughout their lives. And so is ERNIE. But where is he?

INVENTING A MIRACLE WORKER

IS ERNIE IN YET?

Where is the machine we need? After Premium Bonds were announced in April 1956, the challenge was set to work out how the winning Premium Bond numbers could be randomly chosen and selected quickly enough to make the whole thing feasible when millions of pounds were at stake.

Those tasked with inventing a miraculous machine were basing their thinking on the two essential characteristics of any properly functioning prize draw system: complete randomness and high speed selection.

There wasn't much time, but they looked at a number of options, including pulling numbers out of a drum (a giant tombola), or providing a system where nine separate tubes would drop lettered and numbered balls to form the winning number. It quickly became apparent that the length of time needed would be prohibitive. The only solution for a credible prize draw on such a scale in 1956 was an electronic method of picking the numbers.

ERNIE'S LITTLE HELPERS

The team that brought ERNIE to life was part of the Post Office Research Department in Dollis Hill, North London, where the World War II computer, Colossus, had been constructed. Winston Churchill's wartime bunker was built underneath the site and over the main entrance was the inscription "Research is the Door to Tomorrow."[1]

When it comes to important people and machines, there's a line that runs from Enigma to Colossus to ERNIE. It turns out that several members of the team that designed ERNIE were the brains behind the design and construction of Colossus, the machine which sped up the decoding of enemy messages in WW2. Colossus, effectively the world's first computer, was a more powerful version of the more famous Enigma, whose code had been broken by Alan Turing and others. Owing to the Official Secrets Act, even other members of the ERNIE team did not discover the famous history of their colleagues until the late 1970s.

The man behind Colossus was Tom Flowers. The ERNIE team used technology he'd pioneered – the output part of the machine was a direct copy of the circuits in Colossus. Sidney Broadhurst, leader of the team, and Harry Fensom were both involved in the Colossus project. Dame Stephanie Shirley also worked on the first machine, ensuring ERNIE's output followed a random pattern.

When the order came for ERNIE, Sid Broadhurst's team was evaluating the use of transistors in telecommunications. Transistors – a semiconductor device acting as a current amplifier – had been invented in 1947. They were to become the fundamental building block of the circuitry of modern electronics and computers. At the outset of the pop and rock 'n' roll era, Pye had just brought out the first transistor radio for a burgeoning teenage market in Britain.

INSIDE ERNIE

Using the new technique of printed circuits, including 1,500 transistors alongside 1,000 ferrite cores, Sid Broadhurst's team totally transistorized ERNIE's random digit counting, storage and checking. The ferrite cores were small, 2mm magnetic rings used for the counting and storage of the random numbers.

The neon diodes, the source of the random noise, were mounted in specially designed metal tubes suspended on springs with a low oscillation frequency. This ensured that any external vibrations could not affect the source of randomness. To screen them electrically, the metal tubes were then put inside earthed metal boxes and the boxes were mounted on racks, each with four rubber shock absorbers.

The randomness was created by generating noise through a gas discharge neon diode in a vacuum tube. The electrons produced at one end of the diode collided with neon gas as they passed to the other end. The collision between the electrons and the gas produced random noise. This random noise was fed through three amplifier valves which shut off at intervals of one-sixteenth of a second, and this was recorded on the ferrite core counters, which converted the noise into numbers. Each digit had its own noise generator. Every complete nine digit number produced was given a "sister" number and, to add further assurance that the output was random, one complete number was subtracted from the other to give the final winning number. This was then fed into a teleprinter, from which point it was all up to human communication.

With the first draw due in June 1957, the machine had to be up and running months beforehand. For team member, Jack Armitage, it was "a brave decision considering the time scale … This was leading edge technology in 1956 and whilst Manchester University produced a transistorized computer for their own use, ERNIE was probably the first large-scale machine to use these techniques in the public domain in the UK."[2]

In order to maintain belief that a machine could be delivered in time for the first draw, the team produced a non-transistorized electronic demonstration model, showing how a random digit would be generated. It was unveiled to TV cameras on 25th July 1956 by Dr Charles Hill, the Postmaster General, known as the "Radio Doctor" in the Second World War, and who later became chairman of the BBC.

Jack Armitage himself was responsible for ERNIE's Random Noise Generators – the "random source" from which the winning prize numbers would be generated. He knew they had to be beyond criticism.

ROOM C308

The Ministry of Works (MoW) had converted a 90,000 square foot Home Office store in Lytham St Annes into the home of Premium Bonds. In January 1957, five months before the first draw, ERNIE was moved to the new HQ for further testing, as five separate steel cabinets each containing a rack of equipment.

Premium Bonds had gone on sale two months earlier in November 1956. End of year sales already amounted to £55 million. Photocopies of every bond sold were being filed in the Numerical File, a series of rooms, called Spurs, off a central corridor in C Block. ERNIE's home was to be in the centre of this file, in Spur C308.

ERNIE had a teleprinter output selector that would recognize where each number was filed and only numbers filed in that room would be received.

The MoW also built a large wooden platform with a red carpet for the illustrious new resident. ERNIE was re-assembled on 19-inch standard Post Office racks housed inside five steel radio cabinets, each with a lockable door on the front. Altogether, he was about 3.5m long, 2m high and 0.5m wide.

WE'VE GOT THE POWER

Although ERNIE only used about 2 kilowatts of power, he just couldn't afford to depend on the public supply. To fail during the monthly draw was unthinkable. So, ERNIE's engineers installed a "No Break Power Plant" in the room immediately behind him. For a machine designed for randomness, it sounds odd to say it, but nothing was left to chance. The supply came from two alternators - two in case one should fail! A control cubicle enabled the two to be synchronized. Each alternator was driven by a motor. Power for the motors came from the Battery Room where two banks of lead acid batteries were being constantly charged on the public supply. The batteries also provided power for the two "master" and 22 "slave" printers connected to ERNIE.

The mercury arc rectifiers charging the batteries proved to be the most fascinating aspect of ERNIE. The 75cm inverted, pear-shaped glass enclosures emitted a ghostly blue glow, each with three arms arcing electricity into a pool of boiling mercury. If you're thinking Frankenstein, ERNIE wouldn't appreciate it.

In the event of the public supply failing completely, the engineers set up a mobile generator in a building outside. In the event of prolonged mains failure, there was a steel cabinet with 12 one-gallon cans of petrol.

Jack Armitage: "We would now describe this as 'belt and braces' but at the time it was felt there should be no room for failure."!![3]

If it all sounds a bit Heath Robinson today, ERNIE was a technological miracle of his time. He was the first such machine of his type in the world and one of the first examples of an explicit commercial use of this type of technology. And he cost just £25,000 to build.

Weighing in at 1,500kg and the size of a van, ERNIE was fighting fit and ready to rumble.

THE VERY FIRST PREMIUM BONDS DRAW

Over £48 million had been invested in Premium Bonds in November 1956. In those days, you had to hold them for six months to be eligible for the first draw on 1st June 1957. As there had been no previous draws, over 23,000 prizes had to be

ERNEST MARPLES STARTS THE FIRST PREMIUM BONDS DRAW

allotted. To generate the numbers needed to produce these prizes meant that ERNIE would have to run day and night for two and half days with pauses only for meal breaks and paper changes.

The conditions of the first draw were somewhat cramped. Inside the hut were ERNIE and his console, on a platform of five standard Post Office racks, with guard rails. Next to ERNIE, was Postmaster General, Ernest Marples, switching him on to produce the first winner. Crammed into the hut besides both were camera-wielding journalists, TV presenters, members of the National Savings movement, Premium Bond management and Dollis Hill Research staff.

New Postmaster General, Ernest Marples, addressed the packed room, first describing ERNIE as an "electronic 20th century spinning wheel"[4] before becoming more technical: "ERNIE stands for Electronic Random Number Indicator Equipment, but I don't think we can understand it all." Lord Mackintosh, head of the National Savings Committee, apparently chipped in with, "Well, I'm sure I can't if you can't."[5] ERNIE himself said nothing.

Original investors were competing for a top prize of £1,000. They announced a winner after 15 minutes. An investor in Cumbria won the top prize.

The draw continued through Saturday and Sunday until Monday 3rd June at 4.00pm, a total of 55 hours with about twelve hours of stoppages. There were short stops for paper changes on the teleprinters and longer breaks for meals. In the end, 60,000 numbers were drawn at a rate of approximately 2,000 every hour. A rota of engineering staff operated a 12-hour shift system. A member of the Research staff was always available and a bed was provided for him in the next Spur, C307. It took 10 days to complete the draw fully.

The business of finding which numbers match Bonds was done by hand by a team of workers at Premium Bonds HQ. The winning numbers were printed on a gummed tape stuck to a card. Checking it against the Bond numbers in circulation involved trawling through files to find record cards matching the selected numbers.

After that first famous prize draw, ERNIE was certainly the name on everyone's mind. But where did the name come from? According to Jack Armitage: "We don't know who chose the name but 'Indicator' seems to be the only word they had to add. Someone said it was 'a lovely acronym' and 'an easy, solid, down-to-earth name.'"[6]

IT'S A MYTHSTORY...

Q: Who came up with the name ERNIE?

NICE LITTLE ERNIE: It wasn't Sidney Broadhurst, Harry Fensom, Steve Brook, Jack Armitage, Harold Macmillan, Harold Wilson, the Archbishop of Canterbury, Ernest Marples, Bob Hope, Bruce Forsyth, Norman Wisdom, Frankie Howerd, Benny Hill, Judi Dench, Peter Bareau, Alan Cook, Sue Simpson, Tim Mack, Mark Brooks or Jim Northover. It wasn't Winston Churchill and it wasn't me. It's a mystery...

ERNIE TUNES IN AND TURNS ON

And so things remained for years and years and years. Occasionally switched on by celebrities ranging from Norman Wisdom and Bob Hope to Jayne Mansfield and Judi Dench, ERNIE lived a quiet life and simply got on with his job in Room C308 of a prefabricated hut built for wartime purposes.

Until, that was, some time in the late 1960s, when staff decided that the cream-painted brick room needed a bit of a makeover. Tom Watt, a guitar-playing interior designer, arrived on site wearing an ex-fireman's coat and flares. ERNIE's room quickly took on a very different flower power hue. In the spirit of freedom, Watt got rid of the guard rails and painted the room in deep plum, the colour of his jeans. It shocked some members of staff, but nobody could dispute that ERNIE suddenly looked more liberated.

THE IMPARTIALITY OF BEING ERNIE

QUICK OFF THE DRAW

If some people felt ERNIE was rather slow off the draw, they themselves were not. By the end of 1957, 13 million customers had bought into Premium Bonds to the tune of £125 million.

Yet, as early as 1958, some were suggesting that ERNIE was not as impartial as he made himself out to be. The *New Scientist* magazine looked into it and concluded, "There is no chance whatsoever that Ernie at any time in his young life has shown favour for any particular type or number of bond."[7]

The randomness of ERNIE was of the utmost importance and tests on it were carried out by two mathematicians, including Stephanie (Steve) Brook. Later Dame Stephanie, she appeared on a 2004 Radio 4 programme called *Number Cruncher*, in which she described the end product of their statistical work on the randomness of ERNIE by stating that, there was no reason *not* to suppose that these numbers come from a random source. This is the sort of scientific comment that winds up non-believers to fever pitch.

IT'S A MYTHSTORY...

Q: Is it true that ERNIE's randomness today is assured by calibrating his number generating software with figures to the tenth decimal place acquired by squaring the root of the variable amount of methane produced by the UK's cattle population in the days of the preceding month?

NICE LITTLE ERNIE: Just out of interest, the real explanation is even more mind-boggling, but a lot shorter than your question. I have a specialized Intel chipset that uses changes in the voltage and heat energy given off from transistors (thermal noise) as my source of randomness. Clear...?

WHY IS HE SO STOCHASTIC?

As a non-scientist, myself, I've been made to understand quite clearly that the one thing that very few people understand about Premium Bonds is the scientific basis of randomness.

So, let me try to explain it to you. ERNIE is the world's only stochastic machine. Random, uncertain, chaotic. You see, machines are supposed to perform to order and be anything but stochastic. The randomness of electrons and natural unpredictable variance of the physical processes involved in ERNIE mean that systematic trends and similar cumulative effects that affect any pseudorandom number generator are reduced greatly, if not eliminated. Got it?

Journalists have grappled with this for decades. ERNIE's been called a cultural oxymoron, a munificent bingo caller. For one, ERNIE is a model of determinism, but what he is "supposed to do determinably is be interminably indeterminable." [8]

Whatever, the world just has to take the proof of this from independent tests. ERNIE's output is independently tested each

THE CAST OF MINDER WITH ERNIE 2 IN A PROMOTIONAL VIDEO

month by the Government Actuary's Department and the draw is only valid if the output passes tests that indicate it is statistically random. Independent ERNIE has always independently passed every independent test. Without fail. Independently.

BY GAD

The Government Actuary's Department (GAD) carries out this series of statistical tests on ERNIE's results to make sure the numbers generated are not following any kind of pattern, because that would suggest a bias. The four main tests are:

1. Frequency test. Making sure every possible character in every position of the Bond numbers appears as often as it should.
2. Serial test. Looking at how often one digit follows another, e.g. how many 3s come directly after 7s.
3. Poker test. Analyzing how many times a group of four consecutive characters contain four identical characters, how often they contain three of a kind, two of a kind and no matches.
4. Correlation test. Looking at how often characters in two different positions appear in those same positions over a series of Bond numbers.

If no pattern is discernable, the draw is judged to be random and GAD issues a certificate stating that this is the case. The tests have never detected a pattern in ERNIE's selection. Never. Got that? What else will satisfy you? Perhaps if you did the tests yourself...

A CONSPIRACY OF DUNCES

But a society that has grown up watching the *X Files* and reading British newspapers tends to believe the worst about humanity. A machine is only as good as the people who control it. So, there are people out there, in our midst, who don't believe a word that NS&I or government actuaries say about ERNIE's randomness.

This is all very dispiriting for ERNIE. It's not that these people suffer from more than average bad luck, exactly. It seems that they do not seem to accept other people's good luck. And this group of people runs across the spectrum of society, from number dunces to the cast of *Minder* to mathematical geniuses.

All the Government actuaries in the world cannot dissuade self-righteous mathematicians in full flow: "Freak draws must be expected to happen every few years even if ERNIE works as intended and it would indeed be suspicious if the testing process did not sometimes pick them up…There is no point in having a watchdog which never barks."[9] ERNIE has never heard a woof in all his years.

THE FASTEST MILLIONAIRE MAKER IN THE WEST

HOW MUCH LONGER?

There were 48 million Premium Bonds in the first draw. With a Prize Fund Rate of 4%, 23,142 prizes totalling £969,750 had to be dispensed as quickly and efficiently as the technology allowed.

To find that number of prizes, ERNIE had to generate 60,000 numbers so that 23,142 eventually matched. He could only generate 2,000 numbers an hour and every good worker needs a tea break.

Although that first prize draw was exceptional and ERNIE didn't have to find 23,000 prizes a month again until November 1960, it got harder over the years to do things quickly and efficiently.

If he were operating today, the very first ERNIE would take 77 days to complete a draw. In his final year, he was taking 10 days. We all get slower as we get older. Fortunately, this incarnation is well looked after by his new owners, The Science Museum in London. But let's congratulate him on the fact that, between June 1957 and January 1972, he generated numbers for 8,067,575 prizes worth £303,779,900.

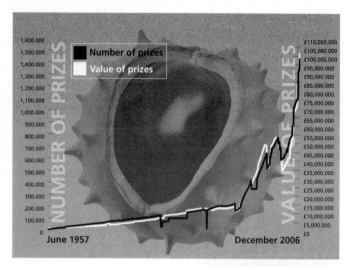

HOW THE NUMBER AND VALUE OF PRIZES HAVE GROWN

- Number of prizes
- Value of prizes

June 1957 — December 2006

ERNIE 2

Twenty million people held Premium Bonds when the new ERNIE came on stream in February 1972. His first task was to dispense 83,416 prizes worth £3,408,100, much more quickly than his illustrious predecessor.

INSIDE ERNIE 2

By using electrons rather than gas, ERNIE 2 was able to produce numbers at a much faster rate than ERNIE 1.

Designed and built by Plessey in Poole, Dorset, ERNIE 2 weighed half of ERNIE 1 at 760kg. Instead of gas, ERNIE 2 used a source of quantum mechanical noise (Johnston noise) generated from a Zener noise diode, which produced random pulses of electrons. As a current was passed through the diode, the randomly moving negatively charged electrons moved haphazardly through the diode to the positive pole. The different pulses produced by the electrons moved counters – one for each Premium Bond digit. The readings on the counters were then recorded and converted into winning Premium Bond numbers.

ERNIE 2 was a far more ostentatious machine than the austere looking ERNIE 1 and was specifically designed to look like one of the sets from the James Bond movie, *Goldfinger*. But *Goldfinger* ran in 1964 and ERNIE 2 appeared in 1972, almost a decade later. Well, think about it, if you go for a night out in your new clothes, you wouldn't expect to be decked out in your Western-influenced Line Dancing gear from the mid-90s, would you?

By the time he was decommissioned in 1988, ERNIE 2 was taking five-and-a-half hours to complete a draw dispensing 190,000 prizes worth £11.3 million. Looking distinctly retro, he was only too glad to join his predecessor in the halls of the Science Museum.

Between February 1972 and August 1988, ERNIE 2 generated numbers for 22,740,704 prizes, worth £1,494,420,100.

ERNIE 3

ERNIE 3 reduced the time taken to run the draw from five-and-a-half hours to two. When popular TV scientist, Professor Heinz Wolff launched ERNIE 3 in September 1988, he made the point that the new ERNIE could produce 330,000 numbers per hour, five times quicker than ERNIE 2 and 165 times speedier than ERNIE 1. Answering people's questions about alternatives, Wolff noted in his irresistible Germanic accent that "to have a roulette wheel big enough to carry the numbers of every bond in issue it would have to be the circumference of the earth."[10]

Developed by Logica CMG, ERNIE 3 weighed 15kg, less than 2% of ERNIE 2.

ERNIE MARK 3 REVEALS THE WINNING NUMBER

Suiting the decade of his birth, ERNIE 3's design style was deliberately "kitsch." He already looked outdated. Built-in tastelessness...hmmm. ERNIE 2 had been a throwback to the 60s, when the country was in the troubled 70s. Perhaps ERNIE 3 was a reflection of the hedonistic 80s when the country was already looking towards the 90s.

INSIDE ERNIE 3

Like his previous two incarnations, ERNIE 3 used a separate noise generator to produce each digit of the Bond number, but the overall hardware that generated the numbers was far smaller.

Like ERNIE 2, Zener diodes were used to produce noise that could be recorded. The diodes produced noise within a bandwidth of 10KHz to 100MHz.

The noise from the two Zener diodes was compared and when the noise from one diode was higher than the noise from the other a random pulse was produced. It wasn't possible to predict when the noise voltage from one diode was higher than that from the other and the pulses produced occurred with random time intervals between them.

Each pulse train was passed to the input of a separate binary counter. A signal was then sent out, allowing the pulses to be counted by each counter for a fixed period of time, one two-hundredth of a second. After each number was read into the store, it was written to two separate magnetic discs within ERNIE 3.

Once all the numbers for a prize draw were generated, the contents of the two magnetic discs were compared to prove that they were identical. Then the discs were copied to CD-ROMs and checks made to ensure the content was still identical. One CD-ROM was used as input into a computer system, which matched the winning Premium Bond numbers with the names and addresses of the winners.

By 2004, the sheer volume of the Bonds in the draw slowed ERNIE 3's performance so much that the time taken to produce 1.7 million numbers for the draw increased to five hours once more. Throughout the dynamic period of Premium Bonds growth in the nineties and early noughties, he had worked flat out. At the end of his lifecycle, he was having to dispense 780,000 prizes worth £47 million.

Before he joined his superannuated predecessors at the Science Museum, ERNIE 3 let the world know that, between

September 1988 and March 2004, he generated numbers for 77,885,566 prizes, worth £5,113,645,250.

IT WASN'T ERNIE'S FAULT THEY LOST INTEREST

In 1999, NS&I announced that a minor administrative error meant a small number of customers would not receive prizes at the time they were due. The press jumped onto it en masse, pointing the finger at the integrity of the UK's most trustworthy random number generator: "Muddled Ernie cheats Premium Bond winners," "Seven die waiting for Bond cash after error," "£350,000 Ernie slip-up," 'Ernie goes on the blink and doesn't pay out.' "Faults with the Premium Bond computer Ernie have led to thousands of bond holders missing out on prizes. City accountants have been called in by officials from National Savings to deal with the crisis, the biggest in Ernie's 43-year history."[11] A Newman cartoon in *The Sunday Times* depicted an angry investor standing next to ERNIE with a sledgehammer, shouting, "Your number's up!" But it wasn't ERNIE's fault at all. He generated numbers as usual, but a human error on a separate operational system meant that a small number of winning numbers were mistakenly marked ineligible for prizes. It affected 815 out of 23 million customers. It was the first and only instance of this happening in Premium Bond history. National Savings apologized to every customer affected and paid compensation for the loss of interest.

ERNIE 3's successor, the very current incarnation of this huge shoulderer of national responsibility, was waiting for me in a dusty, non-descript storage room in the Blackpool home of Premium Bonds. I was all set to meet the fastest millionaire maker in the North West.

MAN MACHINE

THE CHARACTER CALLED ERNIE

HAL, K9, Marvin the Paranoid Android, C3PO. I never got to meet any of them. And now, I've been to the remotest corners of a Thunderbirds-style building in Blackpool that houses this nation's most famous man machine. ERNIE.

Countless voices tell me that ERNIE is not a computer. He cannot be programmed and is not connected to any network (Hey, he's very like me, then!). But he does produce numbers. Perhaps, then, he's a comput*or*. He's not at risk from hackers or viruses. Not that ERNIE was ever just a "machine." Back in the beginning, there was a human touch, "people have faith in him," he gave them "a sporting chance."[12]

I'd read reports about ERNIE being an unassuming piece of kit, not dissimilar to a DVD, but I didn't want to believe it. In Blackpool, I'm really hoping to discover that the face of Premium Bonds is a wizened old man in a granddad shirt, smoking a fag, sitting on an upturned tea chest, reading *Punch* magazine, a mug of Bovril on his knee, pulling strings and pushing a few buttons in a Wallace & Gromit basement.

When the moment comes, I have to go in undercover, on another pretext. Ostensibly, I've travelled up the M6 to meet M1 and M2. Agent Million (M1) escorts me into a dusty, triangular-shaped office used for storing files. I find myself sitting on a red swivel chair, with Agent Million on my left and ERNIE on my right.

ERNIE is: black, shiny, compact and, yes, I feel I could pick him up, take him home and put him under my TV. But I'd leave his monitor in Blackpool. Even my TV screen is wider than that. He's small and somewhat shy. In fact, he uses quite a different version of himself for publicity purposes – the ERNIE Simulator.

ERNIE's famous in his own way, but his celebrity is not about looks. It's what you do in this life that counts. And the real ERNIE is a character. And very definitely a "he," not an "it."

INSIDE ERNIE 4

In 2004, Premium Bonds needed a new machine that could generate 11-digit numbers for the first time.

Designed by Logica CMG, ERNIE 4 is able to use a single random noise generator to produce a whole nine, ten or 11-digit number.

At the heart of ERNIE 4 is an Intel silicon-based hardware random number generator, which uses a random source of thermal noise derived from two free-running oscillators, one fast and one much slower. The thermal noise is used to modulate the frequency of the slower oscillator. This variable, slower oscillator triggers measurements of the faster one, and drift between the two provides a source of random binary digits. Using Delphi code software, a stream of random bits is then converted into Premium Bond numbers without influencing the randomness of the output.

ERNIE 4 weighs 10kg, just two-thirds of ERNIE 3 and one half of one per cent of the original ERNIE.

Unlike the real McCoy, the public face of ERNIE is known as the ERNIE Simulator – a futuristic spaceship cockpit – that is used to demonstrate the draw.

The draw takes him two-and-a-half hours, producing a million numbers an hour.

If ERNIE 1 was still being used today, he would take 77 days to complete a draw, compared with the three-and-a-half hours taken by ERNIE 4.

From his first draw in April 2004 to December 2006 and the 50th anniversary draw, ERNIE 4 had generated numbers for 37,329,993 prizes worth £2,307,005,850 - more than ERNIE 1 and ERNIE 2 put together (and half of ERNIE 3's output).

Not just a persona, but a personality. So, let's forget the speech marks. We're on first name terms. But I'm happy to keep the capital letters. It's a matter of respect. And, over the last 50 years, this thrice reincarnated miracle has produced the numbers for more than 150 million tax-free prizes worth over £9 billion and made 188 people millionaires, as at June 2007.[13] He's generated more chaos and noise than that other great British institution, The Sex Pistols. ERNIE has my eternal respect.

And now not one metre away from my itchy right hand is the CD with ERNIE's latest winning numbers that Agent Million has cross-checked with existing Premium Bond numbers. I feel serious yet silly, like a character from a *Thunderbirds* movie. Except there are no strings attached. And this is Blackpool, rather than a palm-strewn island off the coast of America. What sort of a conversation do you think we have? After all this waiting, what would you ask this character called ERNIE?

AIR MAIL

SPECIAL MAIL FOR ERNIE

Agent Million once went on holiday to Fuengarole and sent a postcard back to ERNIE, with just the words "ERNIE, England" as the address. And, yes, it arrived. Everyone knows ERNIE.

ERNIE, ENGLAND

Here's what ERNIE has to tell me…

He admits he's a chaotic personality. Quite eccentric, in fact. Still, he gets certified by the Government Actuary's Department every month…

Having to carry the responsibility of being "the power behind Premium Bonds" can be quite a burden at times…

Don't get him wrong, they do value him. He is after all their only natural source of entropy in hardware form. When it comes to random number generation, you just can't trust software. It can only mimic true unpredictability and tends to fizzle out into patterns, while ERNIE's robust constitution assures his randomness....

He likes being unpredictable and it has its good points. He gets away with being a noisy bugger and his specialized Intel chipset uses thermal noise from transistors as its source of randomness – changes in the voltage and heat energy given off…

It's incredibly difficult to generate random numbers, yet the older he's become, the easier he's found it to juggle more and more…

It's all very well having captured the nation's hearts, but he's still saddened by the amount of criticism he gets from a vocal minority – you should see the tone of some of the letters and emails! Although he makes lots of people winners, it seems ERNIE himself cannot win…

Dear ERNIE, is something sinister going on in Blackpool? Dear ERNIE, I think I've got you on this one. I read somewhere that there is no test to prove randomness, but that your whole integrity on randomness is determined by a series of tests! Dear ERNIE, you should stop confusing people by talking about probability and randomness in the same sentence. They have no relation, you know. Perhaps there is some skullduggery going on…

Sometimes, ERNIE just wants to disappear into thin air…

ERNIE'S SECRET PATTERN

Disappearing into thin air is not an option at the moment. Finding an escape route just wouldn't be "on brand."

As for the future…

In 1988, when ERNIE 3 was launched, a *Guardian* journalist noticed a curious thing.[14] ERNIE 3 had replaced ERNIE 2 after an interval of 16 years. As ERNIE 2 had replaced the original ERNIE after 16 years. And that journalist wasn't to know that ERNIE 4 would replace ERNIE 3 in 2004, after another 16 years. Every 16 years, ERNIE grows smaller and achieves more. So, there is a pattern to ERNIE after all!

The various ERNIEs have been "cultural signatures of their

times." ERNIE 1? "Functionalism and the sober-minded business of a state-managed saving scheme with perks." ERNIE 2? "Consciously modelled on the James Bond Goldfinger film set…cabinets housing the tape drives were shrouded behind lace curtains, signifying reverence, authority and the mystique of inaccessibility." ERNIE 3? "Part of a game-show setting suggesting, perhaps, the fortuitousness of fortune?"

Well, I've met the compact man machine himself and been inside the very much larger public face of ERNIE 4 – the ERNIE Simulator. Stepping into it is like taking the helm of a large space ship. I can see where all this is going.

A VIEW OF THE ERNIE 4 SIMULATOR

ERNIE 5, 6, 7...

In 2020, when ERNIE 5 should appear on the scene, I think he'll be the size of...well, we probably won't be able to see him with the naked eye at all. He may be the first ERNIE that is part man, part machine. They'll have to feed him on the National Debt.

In 2036, ERNIE 6 will be a speck of bacteria on the surface of the Moon, with a brain even bigger than Marvin the Paranoid Android.

In 2052, ERNIE 7 will be a switch inside your head – which is like saying that we'll all be a number inside ERNIE, just as he will be a number inside us.

Our journey to ERNIE will be shorter than ever. And we'll love him all the more for it.

HAPPY BIRTHDAY, ERNIE!

People at NS&I reckon ERNIE does one thing and that's all he can do. Well, he's made quite an impression on me, I can tell you. So, that's at least two things. And I'm not the only one to be affected this way. He gets birthday, Christmas and Valentine's Day cards. People dedicate poems to him, worry about his health, send Epsom salts, castor oil. On ERNIE's 40th birthday in 1996, a very nice lady sent a card "to the Random Reveller." I've seen the cards, the gifts. They threw their knickers at Tom Jones. They toss Phyllosan tablets at ERNIE.

His Prize Draw Supervisor, Stuart Pilkington, says people think they might get some extra luck by sending him a card but it won't do any good at all – ERNIE has never seen himself as hard-hearted as that. He can't think of anyone who gives as much as he does.

Let's hold on to ERNIE. He's not just a bit of maths and stats for the nerds, some Science Museum nostalgia. He has something for everyone. The National Savings people encouraged this brand personality from the very start. What a good move that was. ERNIE remains an important part of the Premium Bonds brand.

He may not form part of the way it communicates on an everyday basis, but he is its living history, embodying all the security, straightforwardness and integrity that mean so much to NS&I and to us, the public. Through the years, in a faceless world of financial products, ERNIE has helped Premium Bonds retain their human touch. Long live ERNIE!

Notes

1   *Inside Out – North West*, bbc.co.uk, 20th September 2004.

2   Jack Armitage, *Ernie, Son of Colossus*, manuscript in the NS&I archive.

3   ibid.

4   Samuel Dean, "Never been 21 before," NS&I archive paper produced for National Savings, 1978.

5   Jack Armitage, op. cit.

6   ibid.

7   Clifford Ashworth and JA Armitage, "The impartiality of ERNIE," *New Scientist*, 26th June 1958.

8   Benjamin Woolley, "The Uncertain Computer," *The Listener*, 24th October 1988.

9   JL Field, EA Johnston and JC Poole, "The mathematics of Premium Savings Bonds," *The Institute of Mathematics and its Applications Bulletin*, May/June 1979

10 "Meet our Ernie's grandson," *West Lancashire Evening Gazette*, 1st October 1988.

11 Neasa MacErlean, "Muddled Ernie cheats Premium Bond winners," *Observer*, 29th August 1999.

12 Victor Zorian, "The importance of being ERNIE," *Lancashire Life*, March 1961.

13 Between April 1994 and June 2007.

14 Doron Swade, "The three ages of windfall fantasy," *Guardian*, 6th October 1988.

4

THE RENAISSANCE OF A NATIONAL TREASURE

HOW PREMIUM BONDS BECAME A 21ST CENTURY WAY OF SAVING

REBUILDING

THE BRAND THAT TIME FORGOT AND WE REMEMBERED

National Savings & Investments will tell you that there have been four eras with Premium Bonds. The first ran from 1956 until about 1961, the initial launch period which received a huge wave of coverage and attention. By 1961, 13 million people had invested £309 million.

The second phase, by far the longest, ran from the early 1960s to about 1993. This was the era of gradual growth, a period which embedded Premium Bonds in the national consciousness, but nevertheless a fairly quiet period. By the end of 1993, 23 million people held £3 billion.

When I look at Premium Bonds today, I often wonder whether they really need marketing at all, or whether it's really as simple as announcing a few more £1 million jackpots. While there's no doubting the success story of the past five years, for the full context of the renaissance of Premium Bonds, we need to go back 15 years to 1993. This was the beginning of what NS&I calls the Jackpot Era for Premium Bonds. By the end of it, almost 23 million people held £17 billion.

And this, in turn, led to the fourth era, Renaissance, an era rounded off by the 50th anniversary of Premium Bonds, with over 23 million people holding £35 billion Bonds.

OUT OF INFLATION, INTO COMPETITION

It's fair to say that National Savings engineered the beginning of each of these eras, although they never quite knew when they were going to end. Take the second era of Growth. It lasted for 30 years. The last 20 had been years of economic turbulence and a roller-coaster battle with inflation yet produced steady growth for Premium Bonds.

As it is today, the National Savings business was based in Blackpool, Glasgow and Durham, with headquarters in Kensington, London. It's safe to say it had been in the doldrums during these white knuckle-riding, high inflation, boom and bust decades.

But, coming out of the 1991 recession, the financial services industry began to wake up to new possibilities. Banks and building societies that had been able to sell Premium Bonds on behalf of National Savings now stopped doing so - they had their own competitive products to push. In the previous 30 years, the only competitor for Premium Bonds had been inflation itself. Now, the real competition was emerging.

And what a spur to action the Nation Lottery was. Commentators naturally assumed that it would spell the end of Premium Bonds. To National Savings, it was the big wake-up call it needed, a true competitor, and government-backed, too! The world was moving on and National Savings needed to catch up.

When, at the instigation of John Major's government, National Savings introduced new Children's Bonus Bonds and Pensioners' Guaranteed Income Bonds, it raised a few eyebrows about the independence of National Savings.

National Savings had been used by a government already tainted by sleaze for purely political reasons to encourage the savings culture for some key target groups in the UK. As National Savings did not want the reputation of being a political lever of government, something needed to be done.

A PREMIUM BONDS BOOKLET FROM THE MID-70s

Premium Bonds was still the flagship product. Although the Government had introduced the National Lottery, getting rid of Premium Bonds was no longer an option. National Savings had anticipated the Lottery and, by introducing the monthly £1 million prize earlier in 1994, had seen sales rocket.

Rather than get rid of this brand, it was time to make something of it. So in 1996 it appointed Peter Bareau as the new Chief Executive of National Savings, with a remit to do something with the range of National Savings products, including Premium Bonds.

Formerly of Lloyds TSB, Bareau was the first head of National Savings to come from the private sector. Previously, the Director of Savings had always been a civil servant seconded into the job.

He immediately saw an opportunity to revitalize the whole business after years of under-investment.

THE MOST RADICAL SOLUTION

With the 21st century approaching, its processes were very much out of date, although the loyalty and service offered by the staff in Blackpool had remained first class. Bareau put through a solution to obtain the investment and improve the technology that National Savings badly needed. For a public sector organization, it was one of the most radical solutions ever devised.

In 1999, all National Savings operations were put out to a competitive tender for outsourcing through a Private Finance Initiative (PFI) or a Private Public Partnership (PPP), as it was called then. Siemens won the contract and holds it to this day. On 31st March 1999, the National Savings payroll contained 4,000 employees. On 1st April 1999, it was down to just 130 (and no April foolery).

Mark Brooks, Head of Media and PR: "National Savings & Investments is now like a virtual company. This floor at Head Office in Kensington only has a handful of people in it and yet it sells £11 billion of products a year." Just what Peter Bareau had in mind.

WITH GREAT CUSTOMER SERVICE
YOU CAN DO ANYTHING

As we know only too well, outsourcing can affect financial services brands. Customers just do not see where the benefit is to them. Banks and building societies who have outsourced to India have suffered lowered customer perception of their banking experience, forcing some companies to bring their operations back home. Despite their power and massive resources, financial institutions are slow to gauge the public mood.

In the case of National Savings, practically all the jobs and their public sector conditions were retained in their existing locations, in new private sector contracts with Siemens. But in a highly competitive marketplace, it would be difficult for any financial services brand not to offshore some tasks at some point. When this happened at Siemens, NS&I made sure only "routine administrative tasks" were being moved. No customer-facing jobs were outsourced to India.[1]

It was noted in the media, but at one length removed through a private outsourcing company rather than a government department, it didn't raise many eyebrows. Besides, NS&I was known for excellent service and all its customer communications (telephone, post, email etc) were in Blackpool, Durham and Glasgow. It still is and they still are.

REDEFINING

THE "GOOD GUY" BRAND

Part of Peter Bareau's legacy was the rebranding that National Savings began in 1998, with a strategic marketing review, emerging in 2002 with a modern yet appropriate identity and a new name, National Savings & Investments.

This rebranding took a long time, because NS&I wanted to delay the launch to accommodate changes to products and relationships with Siemens and the Post Office and ensure the rebrand was not seen as a purely cosmetic makeover. It seemed to cost a lot of money – over £2 million – yet very little in comparison to the size and "profitability" of the organization or any large business restructure. Yet, apart from some sensible comment in the financial press, which recognized that the figure included advertising, the general media pounced on it, having nothing better to do, now that dotcoms had crashed through the floor.

"People tend to see our products rather than our brand," said Peter Bareau. "We are a giant that has not been sufficiently perceived as the big player that we are in the retail savings market."[2]

The old branding, if you remember, was dark blue and orange and featured a crown. It seemed to represent a different set of values. Or did it? The whole point of rebranding is to re-define or re-affirm a brand's values and ensure that it sends out signals that reflect these values in a contemporary way.

I put it to Sue Simpson, Head of Brand at NS&I, that her approach to brand building with Premium Bonds surely had to be a "softly softly" one. She explained: "The rules are enshrined in law. We have 'integrity' as a brand value. We can't tinker with the basic product too much."

Sue has seen the old and the new. As much as anyone in the institution, she knows what is written in the DNA of this brand. "When we did the values in a formal way back in '98, we wanted the reality of the brand rather than what it aspired to be."

In a world where many brands only "aspire" and have forgotten how to "be," this was a clever place to begin. Research and stakeholder consultation highlighted certain strands: security, straightforwardness, integrity. The only aspirational bit was to hold and deliver these values with a human touch.

More than aspirational thinking, this was inspirational, meeting one of the brand's tougher obstacles head on: a brand that never gets to see its customers. Never mind "touch"! And

Who we are

With more than £73 billion invested, National Savings and Investments is one of the UK's largest providers of savings products to personal savers and investors. We are also a government department and an Executive Agency of the Chancellor of the Exchequer.

Our vision

To be recognised as the UK's leading and most trusted savings and investment organisation.

Our mission

Our overall aim is to help reduce the cost to the taxpayer of government borrowing now and in the future. With this in mind, our single strategic objective is to provide the Government with cost-effective retail finance compared with raising funds on the wholesale market.

Our values

When people think of NS&I, we want them to associate us with:

Security: we offer a unique promise of 100% security, backed by HM Treasury

Straightforwardness: we always use clear, everyday language that is easy to understand

Integrity: we are honest and responsible in everything we do and say

Delivered with a human touch: we treat our customers as individuals and recognise their needs

Our strategy

Direction 2007 is our five-year strategic plan aimed at growing our business through a greater emphasis on our customers and their needs, while still providing cost-effective government funding. More specifically, our plan is to raise a total of £15 billion in net financing and £1.3 billion Value Added between 2003/04 and 2007/08.

Our way

NS&I is committed to a way of working that can be described as:

- Progressive
- Decisive
- Working together as a team
- Straightforward
- Trustworthy

the only personality the brand had ever had belonged to a machine called ERNIE. "We needed to remember that there were real people out there. We needed to think of the customers," says Sue.

In developing the values, the rebranding team had a desired customer experience in mind. A satisfied customer would respond like this: "…I experience a reliable organization which respects me as an individual, makes me feel secure, and offers me straightforward products and services in a way that I can understand. I trust NS&I not to mis-sell or mislead and not to hide behind small print. Where there are restrictions to a product or service they are always clearly explained."

Sue and her team quickly realized that, although the flagship Premium Bond product was a thoroughly British institution, the brand could not promote itself through heritage and patriotism. It had to be about something else. It had to persuade the British public to share its brand values.

There was plenty for Sue and her team to work with. "We are only Savings. No complications of mortgages or loans. You never lose your money. We have an emotional tie that banks don't. We're not full of disclaimers. We're the good guy."

NO DISCO DANCING, DADDY!

Many brands set out on the redefinition journey by concentrating on what they are not rather than what they could be. Brands that set out with what they are, what they believe in, what they are good at, what people like about them, have much more chance of success, because they are working from a set of values that they and their customers understand.

Everything about Premium Bonds said "safe and secure," so that's the brand language they developed. And, for Sue Simpson, there was another important consideration: "We didn't want to be too modern and come across like your dad dancing at a disco."

As often occurs with a brand review of this scale, they found they needed to look at the organization's name. Over the years, it had changed from the Post Office Savings Bank to the Department for National Savings. "National Savings" said a lot, but it didn't say it all.

Fiddling about with a name can be controversial, even when people do not particularly like what they have. Any brand stands a chance of losing a great deal of brand equity – that strange mixture of awareness and belief in a brand. Besides, the media goes to town on anything it sees as smelling of intellectual abstraction or, let's face it, branding. It just hates using what it sees as degrading corporate names.

CONSIGNED TO THE FUTURE

Back in 2002, the precedent for National Savings was very recent and very close to home. Remember when the Post Office and Royal Mail relaunched as Consignia in 2001? The press immediately consigned it to the dustbin of history. But really, the press wasn't only attacking the name. It was everything it thought went with it – poorer delivery rates, rising costs, bad industrial relations, losing public confidence. It quickly rebranded to The Royal Mail Group later in 2002.

At National Savings there must have been some doubt. But then again, they weren't about to do anything too modern. Unlike the Post Office, they discovered that people were very indulgent towards the brand.

Perhaps it was the perennial playfulness of ERNIE that had earned the brand this accolade. It meant they might be able to experiment. But names like "Treasure-e" or "Hedgehog" just would not do it.

Sometimes, you just have to take the public's indulgence for what it is – good will – and not abuse it. And there are many ways of abusing that trust by applying inappropriate solutions to an organization's corporate identity. Try an intellectual or high-art approach – remember the furore over the BA tailfins? Or a pompous and meaningless abstraction that could refer to any old product – remember Prince, the popstar, substituting a symbol for his actual name?

So, National Savings simply changed to National Savings *& Investments,* or NS&I for short. It was thinking beyond Premium Bonds, representing a whole range of different products for different needs. It lent the organization a new credibility, automatically placing it as a financial services brand alongside any other, with products that could form a serious part of your investment portfolio – and, just as important, it was still, obviously, government backed.

But politicians just never seem to get branding, do they? And journalists aren't very far behind. When NS&I launched its new name and identity, it received a barrage of criticism from

MPs of all sides. All accused it of "wasting" £2 million on adding two words to the organization's name. Jim Cousins, Labour MP for Newcastle upon Tyne Central and a member of the Treasury select committee, said: "I do not think it is a silly name, but National Savings is an established brand and it didn't require its name to be changed to make people realize it covers investment products."[3]

NS&I Chief Executive, Peter Bareau, said: "The enhancement of the name National Savings and Investments is a direct result of the transformation the business has undergone."[4]

THE REBRANDING JOURNEY – MPs AND HACKS STILL DON'T GET IT

At the outset of the project in 1998, the rebranding team realized it had a lot of work to do: reassess the brand values; define corporate and brand positioning; develop brand architecture/structure; develop brand identity elements; develop integrated strategy for communication of desired positioning; develop related strategies to ensure operational delivery and cultural alignment consistent with desired positioning. The Brand Implementation Programme worked with partners SBS and the Post Office, as well as five creative and media agencies – Lloyd Northover, EHS Brann, OMD, Citigate Dewe Rogerson, Blue Sky. From the strategic marketing review in 1998, brand values were developed in 1999 and strategic branding options explored. Following research and brand strategy recommendations in 2000, the team moved to sharing the vision with SBS, the Post Office and creative agencies in 2001, agreeing brand values, new name, brand identity and website address and the whole implementation programme. Implementation began in 2002 when the call centre 24/7 service was introduced, followed by website soft launch, first Guaranteed Equity Bond and complete roll-out of the project. From then on, it was all about working with Siemens, partners and stakeholders to make the brand live through an end-to-end customer experience. So, journalists and politicians, please note that this process is going to cost a little more than your monthly expenses allowance.

REDESIGNING THE BRAND

ARE YOU FROM THE AGENCY?

Jim Northover, founder of design agency Lloyd Northover, has been associated with Premium Bonds and National Savings for over ten years, so he's now a kind of brand guardian. "Back then, there was no brand consistency. We bid for designing an Annual Report, met Peter Bareau and got involved in a tender for another contract to help with design. We saw a big opportunity. There was a bigger job than just doing a few brochures. We won it, but didn't change everything overnight."

Today, Lloyd Northover is responsible for all the design and publications work for NS&I, from web to print, point of sale, sponsorship and exhibition materials. It's no sinecure and all achieved by tender that has to go out to market every five years, as with other government agencies. The latest round of this tendering process is now underway, with NS&I not expected to make its decisions until April, 2008. [5]

It's the same for other agencies involved with NS&I, all of whom were reappointed in the previous process back in 2003. EHS Brann does the internal communications and direct marketing and Chick Smith Trott does the above-the-line advertising. OMD does the media planning. On the PR front, The Wrigglesworth Consultancy began working with NS&I in 2003 with a brief to "help make Premium Bonds front of mind," targeting the serious investor. In 2006, Fishburn Hedges took up the challenge.

IT TOOK SOME COLOURED BALLS

Lloyd Northover became involved not long after the National Lottery arrived and made such a huge impact on our lives. This new, different, modern product made Premium Bonds look tired and old-fashioned. Many people thought the Lottery would kill Premium Bonds, but it had the opposite effect. It made people rethink about having a flutter in a "safe" way, especially with the introduction of the £1million prize.

"In a sense, Premium Bonds are the joker in the pack – the upside is you can win dramatically and it's always sitting there. The downside risk is you've got no increase," says Jim Northover. He's aware that there is this big question with Premium Bonds of how do you appeal to the under-40s. To him, it may well be a red herring, with half the population due to be over 40 in about three years' time.

Jim's approach to working with Premium Bonds has been to ask more questions: What are the triggers to buy the product? How do we communicate the product better? How do we make it stand out in branches of the Post Office?

So, Lloyd Northover moved the brand away from black and white to colour. And brighter colours, at that – the idea was to be stronger, more positive, more optimistic, but without being in any way trendy or moving into territory that looks unsafe.

IN A NUTSHELL

Standing back from it all, Jim tries to put it in a nutshell, or should I say a conker shell… "There's a comfort factor in NS&I. So, we based our thinking on, 'How do we make every day familiar?'" It was all about finding a corporate identity that would help people focus on the familiar in life – something that sticks around, suggesting reliability, dependability, day in day out.

For the logo, they looked at incorporating familiar, reassuringly British things – a cupcake, a flower, a beach ball, a cup of tea. "We had a little icon of a yellow teapot, not the old brown betty. Although your mum would have used it, however, for a younger generation brown would have been retro."

The focus was very much on primary colours. "Yellow. The sort of thing you'd get in Habitat. You'd find the primary colours in massmarket stuff anywhere now. It's still comfortable and reassuring, but brighter, more optimistic, more of today."

However, there wasn't as much scope for Lloyd Northover to be too clever or too modern. "There was not much room for retro, for irony or for anything surreal." Perhaps some of National Savings' creative agencies had tended to go OTT, suggesting things like a virtual shop or going for a cruise with your Premium Bond winnings. "We knew we had to be careful not to go down that way. It was not at all glitzy, like the Lottery finger. Everything about Premium Bonds had to be clearly understood for itself."

All in all, there had been years of tactical advertising campaigns, achieving immediate sales tasks but not building a recognizable brand. Where were the links between advertising, direct marketing, promotional literature and other forms of communication?

INCREDIBLE BUT TRUE

In the late 90s, a Premium Bonds campaign featured a series of photographs of bizarre subjects with the caption "Incredible but true." History shows that Premium Bonds people do not tend to anticipate the response they actually get. This time, they got an outraged response. The picture that caused most of the furore featured a donkey's head poking out of a holdall carried by a man. Several people felt strongly enough to call National Savings to say that using a picture of a severed donkey's head was beyond the pail. The organization received another call – from the "actor" in the picture, Maurice Brewer. He wanted to explain how he used to run a donkey sanctuary and how the animal in question was actually a dwarf donkey that he carried around because its legs were so small that walking tired it easily.[6]

FAMILIARITY BREEDS CONTENT

In the beginning, Jim Northover found the business to be risk-averse. The logo had not changed for over 15 years. Replacing the crown motif with the conker nearly brought everything to a halt. "There was lots of resonance about Britishness, the emotional recall of childhood. On the other hand, it was about protection, that spiky outer coating, but inside there's something bright and shiny that comes out with growth and maturity." Indeed, it wasn't a pearl or an oyster. It wasn't even an acorn. You had to be British to get the conker allusion.

What's more, nobody had used the conker. "There were so many images out there, but we couldn't gain them a legitimacy as trademark property." But the conker "was one of those ideas where you had to hang on in to the bitter end."

For Jim, it was all about perseverance and overcoming objections, people living with it. Or as he puts it: "I think it was Bob Worcester who said, 'Familiarity breeds content.'"

Of course, the press had a field day about the cost of it all, but only for a short while. What did the *Sun* say? "Conkers and Bonkers." But there were only ever five complaints from customers. Hardly surprising – look at the sales growth. The next time the tabloid press went to town on logos and branding, NS&I didn't even get a mention. There was simply no argument against it.

NS&I now "owns" the conker and can make a fair claim to being recognized for the ubiquity of its Premium Bonds champagne corks. The beach ball, sliced orange, crusty loaf, gerbera flower, shell, cupcake, stopwatch and other icons now feature as a way of brightening up the subject matter. You get used to them very quickly. They become part of the furniture of the brand, or should I say, livery.

It was when listening to Jim spelling out his approach to bringing this brand into the 21st century that it suddenly struck me how different, in essence, are the National Lottery and Premium Bonds. The one is built entirely on encouraging people to escape their lives. The other is constructed completely on confirming people in the very fabric of their lives. Escapism versus Security. You have a choice.

REDISCOVERING

ROCKET LAUNCHER

Now that the organization had a new name and a corporate identity for the 21st century, it was time for the public to rediscover its flagship product. Everything began to change in 2002, when Peter Bareau left. He'd built it. All it needed now was someone to drive it.

Alan Cook had spent his entire 30 years of employment with Prudential, the insurers, rising to the number two position in the business. The new machine NS&I he inherited was lean, sleek and elegant, but there'd been a savage stock market crash and a bit of a recovery. Increasing confidence was encouraging investors to put their money into a bull stock market and more exciting products at a time when National Savings was still seen as a dinosaur forever associated with the Post Office. There was a lot of awareness-raising, perception-changing and promotional work to be done.

The stock market recovered, but not very quickly and there were several huge financial scandals, from Equitable Life to Enron. The financial services industry had lost a lot of trust.

On top of this, Labour had been returned with greater public spending in mind, meaning that the National Savings & Investments machine had not only to perform but to become a top performer in no time at all. Government funding needs called for a new five year strategy to be put in place in 2003. No pressure, then?

Quite by chance, NS&I products, and particularly, Premium Bonds, became a safe haven for investors, particularly high taxpayers. Alan Cook: "It gave me the opportunity to take what looked like a pretty good proposition to the British public."[7] And Cook's proposition was simple – to make it easier for the general public to buy Premium Bonds and other NS&I products. "Financial products are quite complicated. People's eyes glaze over. I think there's huge scope for the market to make it simpler and more transparent."

What followed was the biggest period of growth in NS&I history. Cook's new strategy was all about growing the business by £15 billion in five years. They achieved it in four.

So, due to the phenomenal growth in Premium Bonds, the current strategy is ending, as I write, in March 2007, a year early. Think about it – a jump from £63 billion to £78 billion – over 20% growth in an organization that is now over 145 years old and whose flagship product, Premium Bonds, was known by everyone but seen by no-one. For anyone who thinks there's no interest in Premium Bonds, this renaissance is a story worth reading about.

Cook's strategy was focused on two approaches. First, to use the organization's flagship products as a lever to revitalize sales of some of its other products, such as Index-linked Savings, and close down poorly functioning products, such as the Ordinary Account. Second, to open up the business to the 21st century saver or investor, using Premium Bonds to publicize this change.

GOOD TIMES

Lighting the blue touch paper, NS&I increased the maximum investment 50%, from £20,000 to £30,000. It was great timing. In 2001/02, people had been stunned by the dotcom collapse and their rapidly disappearing pension funds. But in 2003, savers poured more than £7.5 billion into Premium Bonds, almost double the £4 billion of 2002, and equivalent to 10% of the entire net increase in the amount the nation had saved over the previous 12 months.

The *Guardian* newspaper saw this as "demonstrating that while national lottery ticket sales are flagging, the public's enthusiasm for having a flutter remains undiminished ...growing numbers of people are turning away from share-based investments and savings accounts with relatively poor yields, and instead putting their faith in Ernie."[8]

The reaction at NS&I was one of happy surprise: "It always amazes us whenever we get the monthly sales figures through on Premium Bonds. We fall off our chairs when we see how much money is going into them."[9] No PR spin. A natural reaction. Good old English under-statement. The NS&I approach had begun to develop its human touch.

UNLOCKING BRITAIN'S BEST-KEPT SECRET

But there was more to it. In 2003, with a budget of no more than £50,000, Cook's PR team ran the "Unlocking Britain's Best-Kept Secret" campaign. Quite simply, the objectives were to increase sales, inject fun back into the product and to promote the overall NS&I brand.

Besides the normal messages – that Premium Bonds were a serious yet fun investment with the excitement of tax-free prizes, 100% secure, always retaining the original investment – there was something new. The idea was also to assert to the 25 to 45-year-old generation that Premium Bonds were part of the financial fabric of the nation. For such a low key brand to get on the radar of a new audience, this was quite something.

How did they do it? The idea was to get into the first ten

pages of the *Daily Telegraph* rather than the business pages. They were also looking at TV and online coverage. So they put all their thinking into a year-long campaign, using the unique features of Premium Bonds.

THE RISK OF A SUCCESSFUL PR CAMPAIGN

For NS&I, there was one big risk in stretching the coverage of Premium Bonds beyond the personal finance media and into the consumer media. Making Premium Bonds populist could destroy the carefully crafted positioning around "serious investment." For example, announcing the million pound result in a regular slot on radio or TV would attract people who wanted to invest the minimum rather than those who would veer towards the maximum. And, when those minimum holders did not win – though some small holders have won big prizes – that would attract negative comment. There was nothing to be gained by straying into the territory of the National Lottery. NS&I had carefully repositioned Premium Bonds as the "Lottery for Middle Britain." You needed £100 to play and over 300,000 people had the then maximum 20,000 chances a month. The promotion of Premium Bonds had to stretch, but only into the quality mainstream consumer media market. And this had to be done via PR tactics including reaching out to TV and radio. Quality, rather than quantity. In the end, a successful PR campaign would be judged on how well NS&I maintained the "serious investor" positioning for Premium Bonds.

As we've seen, the uniqueness of Premium Bonds often centres around myths. Mark Brooks: "Myths? From a PR perspective, while saying they're not true, they add to the charm of Premium Bonds. They perpetuate the fun element. People discuss them with other people, probably more so than any other form of savings or investment. We've done research that shows 90% of people never discuss personal finance with friends, but a whole lot more discuss Premium Bonds. They're a regular topic of conversation at a dinner party."

Get it talked about! So, here we have a brand that works hard to reject some myths and build others while communicating an overall method of simplicity. Hmmm…little wonder that the web financial forums are full of scrooge-like curmudgeons and conspiracy enthusiasts who think NS&I speaks with a forked tongue. Still, there's always somebody to put them right.

IT'S A MYTHSTORY…

Q: Isn't it true that I would have to live in the South East of England to win the big prizes?

NICE LITTLE ERNIE: Just out of interest, this area of the country holds more Premium Bonds, so more of the winners are likely to be living there. I've done a special analysis which shows that each region receives the fair share of prizes based on the corresponding number of eligible bonds. If you moved to the South East of England tomorrow with your current holding, you would have exactly the same chance of winning as you had in last month's draw, wherever you currently live. I understand that people down there are not as friendly but tend to have more money and, on average, more Premium Bonds. But, I'm from Blackpool, I prefer it up North. I'd stay where you are, if I were you…

SIMPLIFYING THE MESSAGE, DEEPENING THE MYSTERY

The whole "Best-Kept Secret" campaign was based around the monthly announcement of the £1 million prize. They knew this was the lure, so Mark Brooks invented the "Agent Million" persona – the first for Premium Bonds since ERNIE himself.

Lonely after all these years, ERNIE was only too happy for a sidekick. The team built some mystery around Agent Million. Mark Brooks: "Agent Million is like a female Doctor Who. She keeps regenerating. We've now had four. Because this person can change, the image still maintains it." NS&I ensured that, besides delivering the prize in person, Agent Million was available for radio broadcast and print interviews.

The campaign picked up pace because the team was proactive in lobbying for regular coverage of the monthly winning number announcement. They used Ceefax and Teletext. They knew their audiences, successfully targeting GMTV for its large morning audience, and Classic FM, with its age profile. They secured regular announcement slots for the monthly £1 million prize with GMTV, Classic FM, the *Daily Mail, Daily Telegraph, Guardian* and *Daily Mirror.*

However, a national campaign on such a scale had to make some gestures towards populism. For the first time, the team used case studies of Premium Bond holders and winners. Before 2002, legislative restrictions over privacy had made this impossible. Now, however, the media relations team could send publicity agreements to customers which circumvented the restrictions when they returned them signed. The media lapped up the chance to use case studies of large prize winners who did not mind the publicity. As early as January, 2003, a £50,000 winner featured in the women's magazine, *Best.*

Wherever they could and whenever they had to, Mark's in-house PR team made the most of the interest in ERNIE as a number machine with a history of reincarnation. They allowed any nostalgia around Premium Bonds to surface and used it. They focused on ERNIE's 100 millionth prize winner. They attended to important details and showed that they understood what people were saying about Premium Bonds – NS&I created a tracing service for unclaimed prizes and researching and publishing the "luckiest" towns. They used mini-campaigns in the Annual Report and record sales figures announcements to ensure that the business and personal finance media promoted the message.

Although Premium Bonds was a national brand, NS&I recognized the local importance. Mark Brooks: "We sent out 60 press releases that August – one national and one per county." And it doesn't get more local than "personal." They sent factsheets to local radio stations – "ERNIE's Top Five Facts About Premiums Bonds In Your Area." They ran monthly photocalls for local media in each £1 million jackpot area, making sure that their regional press releases contained locally relevant information. These photocalls secured interviews with numerous regional TV, radio and print outlets. In doing so, they became the good news story for everyone to cover. They became the most covered savings brand in the country.

But did this coverage translate into the results they were seeking for Premium Bonds? Yes. The "serious investment" message increased by a factor of three and the "secure" message by a factor of 15 in print coverage through 2003.[10]

"Unlocking Britain's Best-Kept Secret" campaign won the Chartered Institute of Public Relations (CIPR) Corporate and Finance campaign of the year, followed by other awards for direct mail and advertising campaigns.

LAND OF HYPE AND GRAVY

The 2003/04 Annual Report opening proposition stated: "During the last financial year, National Savings & Investments worked hard to improve products and services for our customers and made it easier for them to save and invest with us."

One of the triggers for buying is accessibility. When Cook took over in 2002, NS&I sold more than 90% of its products through local Post Office branches. Things needed a nudge. In March 2003, when ERNIE handed out his 100 millionth prize, investors could now check if they had won anything online, but they were still only able to buy Premium Bonds if they filled in a form and posted it off to NS&I.

Good news stories helped the campaign. In July 2004, NS&I paid a £1 million jackpot to an investor whose £17 worth of bonds were bought in 1959, bucking the trend for maximum bond holders to win the prize and underpinning the whole idea of randomness.

The sheer volume of Premium Bonds in the system, however, meant that ERNIE 3 was taking five and a half hours to complete the monthly draw. So, it was clearly time for another reincarnation. ERNIE 4 was unveiled in August 2004 at London's Science Museum.

ARE YOU BEING ACCESSED?

But development opportunities were still there. And the Big Bang for Premium Bonds happened in 2005, with the launch of a new website designed by Lloyd Northover to reflect NS&I's relevance to the modern saver and investor, and built by Wheel, NS&I's digital development partner. In February, NS&I could finally announce that Premium Bonds were available for buying online.

John Prout, NS&I Sales Director, said: "People with money to save or invest are often pressed for time to sort out their finances. An online resource makes it much easier for customers to save when it suits them, in their lunch break or in a few minutes at the weekend."[11]

In June 2005, NS&I announced that two £1 million prizes would be available from the August draw onwards, allowing people just enough time to buy Premium Bonds to qualify for it. The media pointed out that the value of the prize fund had risen from £14.6m in April 1994 to an estimated £72.4m for August 2005 (meaning you have less chance of winning, due to odds increasing from one in 15,000 to one in 24,000). But they also noted that "the prize fund rate will increase from 3.20% to 3.25%...As the prizes are tax-free this is the equivalent of 5.42% for a higher rate taxpayer and 4.06% for somebody on the basic rate ... Premium Bonds are now considered a significant part of a well-balanced portfolio."[12] For NS&I, this was a well-balanced message, indeed.

And the message had become everything. Jim Northover: "The aim was to change the tone of voice, from self-deprecating and under-stated to straightforward, confident, more expressive. We were looking for a tone of voice that resonates and sounds up to date. Who could speak like that?"

YOU'RE HIRED – THE ALAN SUGAR STORY

While it took years for the brand to arrive at Sir Alan Sugar, it was the clear strategy for NS&I brand communications that helped them identify their man. Simplify. Modernize. Diversify.

SIR ALAN SUGAR

Differentiate. Don't go down the nostalgia route too much. Establish some brand icons. Someone with credibility.

Sir Alan Sugar. Blokish, respected, strong. Very self-contained as a person.

As often happens when your advertising features a celebrity, it quickly becomes personified by them. When I say "Premium Bonds" to people, the majority automatically respond "Alan Sugar." It's a big responsibility!

FROM WALLPAPER TO WILLPOWER

Tim Mack, Head of Marketing and Communications at NS&I, told me the story. "We needed to surprise people. We were wallpaper. Everyone knew who we were and no-one had seen us. We had a latent brand strength that needed to be unlocked. The Sir Alan Sugar ads were the first time we'd been on TV for six years. I reckoned we needed about £4 million of TV advertising a year, considerably less than the competition and based on our latent strength. We launched the ads at a time when we'd added a second £1 million monthly prize. The cost was tiny compared with the billions we brought in."

In fact, it was a £6 million multimedia campaign that ran between June 2005 and January 2006, airing on national TV, radio and in the press. The first TV ad featured Sir Alan in a horse-racing setting, effectively saying that Premium Bonds offer you the chance of winning a lot of money without the risk of losing.

With the ads first appearing one whole year ahead of the 50th anniversary special draw, the timing turned out to be just right, even though the business was still working on itself and its products. Tim: "We'd just launched online. We'd hardly spent any time telling people we were not part of the Post Office. We were still like their internal brand."

But if they hadn't done it, Tim Mack believes that "a lot of money now in Premium Bonds would have gone into instant access savings accounts, the big growth area."

IF PREMIUM BONDS WERE A CAR...

...They'd be a Volkswagen Golf. Or at least according to the Financial Service Industry's 2006 Marketer of the Year, NS&I's Tim Mack. "They evolve, yet carry on from the previous model. Most car life cycles aren't like that. It's also for everyone – in a more restrained and understated way than the Mini." Formerly in the car industry, Mack can wax even more lyrical in his comparison with Premium Bonds. "With an Aston Martin, your feelings and emotions go back to before you could even drive, to your very childhood. With Premium Bonds, we, too, have had to re-earn people's attention a second time around."

The Alan Sugar phenomenon took over. But how did they find him? And how did they get him? Tim: "Alan Sugar was our man from the start. Even if people don't like him, they respect him. He has a particular kind of human touch."

NS&I had prepared a brief to find the person who ended up being Sir Alan Sugar. It had to be a respected, no-nonsense person. In preparing the list, he came out spontaneously, due to his performance on *The Apprentice* TV programme. It's easy to say this in hindsight, but some of the other names on the NS&I list just do not seem to fit the bill. Simon Cowell. Gordon Ramsay. Jeremy Clarkson! You're fired!

A CLEAR, POWERFUL MESSAGE

In a straw poll, Sir Alan Sugar clearly came out top. Tim Mack: "We approached him and our judgement of how he was perceived proved more true than possible. He knew the products, wanted to promote them, wanted to give his fee money to the Great Ormond Street Hospital and insisted on making this clear in the ad. He wasn't being bought."

You can't buy Sir Alan Sugar, but you can buy what he represents, i.e. the Sir Alan Sugar brand. And, with him fronting it, your brand becomes the Sir Alan Sugar brand. Perhaps this was why it was still such a big decision.

The sales were phenomenal. It's not as if the ads were difficult to shoot. "We've only ever done two shoots with him. Just a white desk in a white room. We varied the script. It didn't take long. We said we'd run it by him before going on air."

TALK ABOUT A DIFFERENCE

Has Sir Alan Sugar made a difference in branding terms, rather than just sales? Alan Cook and Jane Platt wrote him letters, thanking him for his support and letting him know how much sales and awareness had gone up. He substantiated Premium Bonds and enabled the brand to promote the telephone and online channels that differentiate it from the Post Office.

Media commentators loved it, give or take the obvious few who needed no excuse to take a swipe at Sir Alan. And Tim Mack is still buzzing with it all: "You know, Virgin is the only example where the person – Sir Richard Branson - makes a difference. But this is financial services. Now we've got advocates and a new kind of person buying Premium Bonds. A lot of self-employed professionals have re-introduced themselves to the brand."

It's almost as if Premium Bonds have found themselves a new set of brand values – comfortable, safe, feel-good, ethical. But Tim Mack knows that it's more than the Sir Alan Sugar factor: "We've sold more Premium Bonds in the last five years than in the previous 45 because we were on an upward trend when we brought in Sir Alan Sugar."

What do you remember of those ads? Here's what I recall: nothing in particular about the product, just Sir Alan making a big point about publicly insisting his fee went to the Great Ormond Street Children's Hospital.

This says as much about the nature of Premium Bonds as it does about Sir Alan Sugar. It suggests that he dislikes the in-your-face hard sell. There is something here about integrity and – despite Sugar's directness - the whole understated nature of Premium Bonds. It's a brand that doesn't like to talk about itself much. It's a brand that's constantly surprised by its own success.

This isn't so much a lack of confidence in the product (far from it) as an under-estimation of the role British consumers play. And, of course, better an underestimation than an overestimation.

THE MECHANICS OF PB50

For those interested in the mechanics of the wider marketing campaign, PB50 is worth looking at.

NS&I began promoting the 50th anniversary of the launch of Premium Bonds during its BBC Proms In the Park sponsorship, following it with the Sir Alan Sugar TV advertising campaign on 1st October 2006. This gave people one month to buy new Premium Bonds for entry into the special 1st December draw featuring five £1 million prizes. The ad actually promoted anniversary draws in December 2006, the launch, and June 2007, the first draw.

NS&I ran a campaign across direct mail, TV, online and press, working with agencies EHS Brann and Chick Smith Trott. NS&I posters and displays in branches of the Post Office were supported by a major Post Office promotion. Tim Mack: "We wanted to drive sales and create excitement around a product that was radical 50 years ago and still is now. We had run integrated campaigns before and knew that any Direct Response Marketing would be uplifted by TV work."[13]

The integrated campaign covered every aspect of buying Premium Bonds. With the 50th anniversary of the launch of Premium Bonds as its focus, it was aimed at all adults and had four aims: to raise awareness of National Savings & Investments; to demonstrate the benefits of investing with NS&I; to encourage potential customers to invest with NS&I directly and through the Post Office; to position NS&I as a different option for financial investments. The leading message was "serious investment."

When shown during the day, the TV ads created by Chick Smith Trott encouraged people to buy via phone or through the Post Office. In the evening, they drove viewers online. As for direct mail, existing customers received mailings inviting them to buy more Premium Bonds. If you received a pack, you might remember the gold lettering on the envelope which made it feel like an invitation to a celebration.

NS&I put banner ads and "skyscrapers" on ten specialist money sites and large lifestyle portals such as Motley Fool and MSN, with a total reach of 14.5 million people. They also spent £50,000 on search marketing.

As far as press ads were concerned, NS&I returned to the titles they knew provided a good response – such as the *Mail* and the *Telegraph*. While a highly targeted local radio media relations campaign achieved coverage on 63 stations, reaching an audience estimated at 5.1 million.[14] NS&I achieved over 200 separate pieces of TV and radio coverage in just 24 hours around 1st November. BBC Radio Lancashire broadcast their entire afternoon show on 1st November from ERNIE's home in Blackpool. The fifth most-read page on BBC website on 1st November was about a Premium Bonds millionaire – NS&I had never achieved that level of pick-up before.

And the results? It's well documented that NS&I had a record sales month for Premium Bonds in October 2006, at £2.2 billion. Much more than double a typical month. Of this amount, they were able to measure that £177 million was attributable to the mail pack, with £99 million coming from search. But the huge uplift in direct and Post Office sales is attributed internally to an integrated campaign across all media.

FROM ORDINARY TO SPECIAL

The past 15 years have revealed that, as far as Premium Bonds are concerned, there is a light that never goes out. And the institution now known as National Savings & Investments has proved that there is a special brand beneath a once faceless, civil service exterior.

How do people experience it? Can you see it? Can you touch it? There's a genuine sense of values. And what values they are!

Those who worked on the rebranding asked all the right questions. What have we got? How will the brand work now? Will people be buying the same product? What, exactly, are we re-launching? A conker? A new name? More like a very successful savings product and a revitalized national treasure for the 21st century.

Notes

1   "Premium Bonds jobs move to India," BBC Online, 17th August 2004.

2   Rupert Jones, "The sleeper awakes to ISA," Guardian Unlimited, 27th March 1999.

3   Phillip Inman, "Two words on National Savings cost £2m," *Guardian*, 12th February 2002.

4   ibid.

5   Noel Bussey, "National Savings kicks off all-agency review," *Campaign*, 19th January, 2007.

6   Sue Beenstock, "Truth stranger than fiction for NS," *Marketing*, 1st October 1998.

7   Nick Mathiason, "The man who saved Premium Bonds," *Observer*, 14th August 2005.

8   Rupert Jones, "Savers stake a double on Premium Bonds," *Guardian*, 18th December 2003.

9   Nick Mathiason, op. cit.

10 Lynne Roberts, "IPR Excellence Awards: Winner – Corporate & Financial – NS&I reinvigorates its Premium Bond brand," *PR Week*, 23rd July 2004.

11 Sandra Haurant, "Premium Bonds go online," Guardian Unlimited, 9th February, 2005.

12 Miles Brignall, "Premium Bonds to pay £1m twice a month," *Guardian*, 18th June 2005.

13 Claire Foss, "NS&I – Bonds make a huge comeback," *Marketing Direct*, 4th January 2007.

14 *Summary of Coverage for Premium Bonds 50th Anniversary Broadcast Campaign*, Markettiers4DC.

5

SURVIVE AND PROSPER
THE FUTURE OF A
NATIONAL TREASURE

THE FIFTH ERA OF PREMIUM BONDS

WHATEVER NEXT?

Launch. Growth. Jackpots. Renaissance. Now for the fifth era of Premium Bonds. What a recovery! But history shows that a recovery can't last forever. What happens next? What is the future for this powerful brand called Premium Bonds and its parent brand called National Savings & Investments?

My betting is that, just as long as ravens stay in the Tower and frogs bonk in my fishpond in spring, Premium Bonds will be with us. The beautiful thing about Premium Bonds is that they are a unique halfway house between saving and spending. By and large, the British public has a need to look after the future while gambling away the present. You can do one or the other with pensions, bingo and the National Lottery. You can do both with Premium Bonds.

TV PERSONALITY, JOHNNY BALL, CELEBRATES THE 50TH ANNIVERSARY OF PREMIUM BONDS

The technology and culture have changed. The product has not. Premium Bonds are a never-changing part of a British culture that's constantly changing. OK, you had Captain Mainwaring, we've got Andy Pipkin. But a changing culture does not necessarily mean one that is getting worse or losing its values.

The product may not change but its benefits certainly do. At present, the "advantage," if we want to call it that, lies with people who put in the maximum £30,000. They are odds on to win prizes. Yet plenty of other people, who do not have £30,000 to dispose of, the vast majority, see other reasons for staying in, either for the short or long term. Investment is a combination of the rational and the emotional. And nobody can take away from this.

Premium Bonds have never been about the Viv Nicholsons of this world. Unless NS&I raises the top Premium Bond prizes to National Lottery and Euromillion levels, the ethos will continue to be about making positive changes to your life rather than throwing it all away, escaping and starting again.

THE FUTURE
FOR SAVINGS

TAKING MORE INTEREST

The exhaustive 2005 Mintel report on attitudes to saving[1] came to some useful conclusions for our future, so let's list them here:

- The necessity to save can only be expected to increase.
- Savings institutions need to engage with their customer base.
- The regulatory regime may help to restore consumer faith.
- Tackling financial capability is likely to move further up the savings agenda.
- Simplifying the tax system may encourage more people to save.

There's great pressure on all of us to do the right thing with savings. People want to save. They just don't find any aspect of it very easy. In the end, it's just not interesting enough for many people to take interest in it, or from it.

It's little wonder that people switch off and look for simplicity. How can you have a relaxing read of a Sunday newspaper, when its fattest section is telling you that your neighbours are laughing at you because you're in a mortgage trap, you bank with the wrong people and you're paying the taxman too much?

So, what?! Stop harassing me! Is it only the nerds who are constantly on the websites looking for the best deals or selling their underwear on eBay? Or are we all at it? Were friends or hobbies a 20th century thing? Leave me alone, I'm not going to spend half of my waking life searching for better deals. Not everyone wants to run faster to save £2 on their electricity bill. Ever felt that way?

Some of us want to save money now. Some of us want to save for the future. Quite a lot of us just want to pay the going rate and enjoy the peace of mind that comes with not being obsessed with money. We just want something clean, clear and simple where we don't have to worry about all that stressful interest nonsense, especially if it offers us an incentive such as the chance of winning something. Hello, Premium Bonds.

SMALL CHANGE

Governments find they are in a bind over saving. It is a hard message to sell.

Whatever the answer, Premium Bonds and a number of other products offered by NS&I operate by communicating their benefit of tax-free savings and investments. We all like a bit of relief.

But what we save we seem to spend. As government after government has discovered, saving is just not as interesting as buying and selling. Yet a big reason why our savings levels are lower than they used to be is not so much the obvious one that

INDEX LINKED SAVINGS CERTIFICATES, ALSO KNOWN AS INFLATION BEATING SAVINGS

we are spending more, but the fact that much of what we are spending is borrowed. The credit generation did not figure in Harold Macmillan's 1950s thinking about the need for thrift and caring for the future.

But there are some good signs that we are actually re-establishing a new savings culture, in parallel to the borrowing culture, based on the acceptance of credit, or debt, as it should more actually be known. The traditional equation of saving versus spending needs tweaking to understand the way we live today. It's also saving versus borrowing.

BIG CHANGE

However, governments must persist. The current government is working on breaking down your barriers, trying to educate you in the ways of financial capability. Despite all the pressures, incentives and hand-holding, some of you are just not with it, not in the frame at all – not heeding the Financial Services Authority's advice and becoming "financially capable consumers" who know when and how financial institutions can help them; less prone to buying products that don't suit your needs, and more inclined to engage proactively with the financial services sector.[2]

Be told! As we've already noted, there is no such thing as a free hunch, lunch, bunch of coconuts. So, wake up and feel the crunch. Your ability to be more financially capable will determine your level of prosperity. Ask your kids. The National Strategy for Financial Capability is beginning at school. Kids are going to be more financially astute than you by the time they're in Year 2. Clearly, what you don't know will hurt you! And that applies to people who own Premium Bonds, too. The number of people who do own them is amazing. But the number of people who moan about Premium Bonds is legend. Most of this complaining is based on myth and ignorance.

How come people persist in this ignorance? How come they prefer to believe in conspiracy theories rather than the information presented to them by NS&I? What are they doing about it? How are they attempting to influence this brand?

The Association of British Insurers hit the nail on the head: "Information is the essential currency of good markets. If people know, they have the potential to act; if they don't, they can't. If they can't act, their preferences cannot influence the behaviour of suppliers."[3]

THE FUTURE FOR PREMIUM BONDS

WHY ARE THEY STILL HERE?

Because there's nothing quite as uncertain as the future, we need to ask a couple of fundamental questions. Why are Premium Bonds still here? According to Jim Northover: "Because nothing completely overtakes anything else."

The way Jim sees it, circumstances will change. The brand is strongly related to how the economy changes. What are people worried about – losing what they've got, or yearning for more? It's a cycle that will happen all over again. For a lot of people, Premium Bonds become attractive because other things become less attractive. The brand will outlive others trying to follow the market, trying to be the next best thing.

The key is always relevance. If the product and the positioning become irrelevant, Premium Bonds will lose out. "The future will be better arrived at by not changing too much and not being seen to try too hard."

NATIONAL TREASURES, HOW WE LOVE THEM!

Dame Judi Dench, Kenneth Williams, Dame Shirley Bassey, Robbie Williams...Robbie Williams?! The point here is that, as a brand, Robbie Williams tries so hard, whereas Premium Bonds, as a brand, does not. Robbie is rich and sad beyond his wildest dreams and may soon fade from the nation's treasure trove. Premium Bonds are richer and gladder beyond their wildest dreams yet cannot afford to be seen as such or try too much. As long as they don't overdo it, they will keep the Midas touch.

Premium Bonds aren't going to disappear. If anything happens to jeopardize the integrity of the draw, or the balance of elements around the Prize Fund, the whole 145-year NS&I house could come tumbling down. There is a reputational risk.

Yes, they had that when they were a quieter brand. Now that they've stood up and spoken for themselves, that risk is higher.

SHOT BY BOTH SIDES

Anyone concerned with a very successful brand will occasionally experience a cold shiver running down their spine. When will our sales reach a plateau? And what then? Will the pressure come first from government or the British public?

Let's face it, in Premium Bonds, NS&I knows it has a very good, very popular product. But not a perfect product. They still attract lower income groups with very little spare cash, on the grounds of being a safe bet, with your money back. But with the minimum purchase now set at £100 it makes you wonder just how appealing Premium Bonds will remain to this group.

Then there's the other end of the scale. NS&I Head of Media and PR, Mark Brooks: "There is an artificial cap. We have a limit on what people can invest. Some people want us to go further." This isn't surprising, with prizes being tax-free, they do benefit higher rate tax payers overall. There is a big temptation to open up to a market that is ready and waiting.

But what will this do to the perceptions of the vast majority who already feel that prizes are skewed towards the rich in the City and south-east in general? And it would be facile to assume that other financial institutions – who also want this market – would stand idly by and watch NS&I clean up through something as simple and easily understandable as Premium Bonds. The gloves are off – certainly since 1999, when National Savings launched its ISA and went head to head with the banks, building societies and investment houses for the first time.

GET THE BALANCE RIGHT

As far as the public is concerned, Premium Bonds may be a simple product. But their management requires an important set of checks and balances to be analyzed and followed carefully. We see what happens when there is a major international event, such as 9/11, or the recent fears over the

Chinese economy. There is panic selling in the equities markets. Premium Bonds are important in paying off the National Debt. They, too, need bolstering against panic selling or any great movement in the market.

Managing the relationship between the rate of inflation, the total amount of Bonds invested, the Prize Fund rate paid back to the public and the odds of winning is a complex one. Where do you even begin? On the one hand it starts with the Bank of England base rate of interest. On the other, it's about how many prizes are being handed out to satisfy the customers. And the interest rates of commercial competitors always have to be considered.

In the meantime, the public's appetite for millionaire status knows no bounds. The prospect of five £1 million prizes in December 2006, even at astronomical odds of winning, brought record sales. NS&I upped the Prize Fund rate to accommodate the three extra £1 million prizes. The odds of winning are still pegged at 24,000–1. How many times can NS&I increase the Prize Fund rate and still keep the balance right?

There have been some public murmurs that odds of 24,000–1 are too high. People perceive that you need to have at least £24,000 in to have a strong chance of a return over the years. And many people just do not have that kind of money. Premium Bonds are not the people's lottery, but there is a historical sense of fairness over 50 years of tradition. Is there perhaps the beginning of a feeling that Premium Bonds are not giving enough back?

There shouldn't be. The Prize Fund rate has been going up steadily for the last six months. As has the total investment in the fund. The Prize Fund Rate is keeping pace with increasing inflation and, because there are more prizes to give away, the odds have been kept at 24,000–1.

NO PUBLICITY, PLEASE

Can Premium Bonds really give more back to the public than they already do? There are only so many £1 million prizes and only so many millions of ordinary prizes to dispense. In the end, you can keep tinkering, but if you are more and more successful, you will attract the wrong kind of attention. Once a brand raises its head above the parapet...well, you finish the sentence.

Whatever NS&I does, Premium Bonds will always be a powerful part of this organization. Younger generations may not yet "get it," but they could if NS&I makes the most of the current publicity around Premium Bonds. NS&I will always need a balanced set of products appropriate to their time. Now that Premium Bonds has shot up in the public's consciousness, it's a classic opportunity for cross-selling.

Strange as it may sound, the fifth era of Premium Bonds may be less about Premium Bonds and more about the future for National Savings & Investments. This may be the time for NS&I to deflect attention away from its flagship brand and onto its wider range of products. It's here that it can be imaginative and competitive enough to give back to the British public what it expects. I expect to see Premium Bonds featuring in publicity in which they draw attention to sister products and different kinds of benefits.

IT'S A MYTHSTORY...

Q: Are Premium Bonds going to be around in 2020 and beyond?

NICE LITTLE ERNIE: Just out of interest, I've survived Harold Wilson's "squalid raffle" claims, the Suez Crisis, Harold Macmillan's Profumo sex scandal, and pipe-smoking, Benny Hill's chart-topping song about a randy milkman, Margaret Thatcher's handbag, the Big Bang, John Major's National Lottery, the dotcom collapse, Noel Edmonds, Big Brother and three reincarnations that would test Dr Who's staying power. The super-casino holds no fears for me. I'll be there for you – you just concentrate on hanging onto your marbles...

THE FUTURE FOR NATIONAL SAVINGS & INVESTMENTS

THE ANSWER IS RIGHT UNDER YOUR NOSE

Go back to the question I asked you in the very first chapter of this book. "If you were working in marketing communications at NS&I, where would you apply your thinking?" Basically, the Ipsos MORI poll in question was about awareness of NS&I rather than Premium Bonds. It used knowledge of Premium Bonds to discover awareness of NS&I.

This was the evidence that supported current thinking about just how much work needs to be done on the public's consciousness.

As you might expect, it's doing quite well with its existing customers, but there is still room to tell one in three of the range of other products it offers. Head of Communications, Tim Mack: "People have 1.1 product holdings with us. One in ten of everyone who holds a Premium Bond also has another of our products. The other nine represent an opportunity."

In 2005, NS&I appointed EuroDirect to help it improve its understanding of a 27 million-strong customer base so that it can communicate better with customers and ultimately develop new products and channels. [4]

NS&I holds over 65 million customer records. Visit Blackpool and the Siemens staff talk about the constant task of "cleaning," enhancing and consolidating the records, to provide a single view of the customer. Forget about Big Brother. This process is all in your interest. In 2006, SIS and EuroDirect won a national award for the work.

CAN I BORROW THE SHIRT OFF YOUR BACK?

On the other hand, the Ipsos MORI research showed that three-quarters of people in this country do not know anything about NS&I or its range of products. In its 2005/06 Annual Report, NS&I said it had doubled its brand awareness and Marketing magazine put NS&I in its top 20 rankings for increased advertising awareness. When it comes to being the "voice" of financial investments, however, NS&I is moving in the right direction, but has a long way to go.

The flagship product is now once again recognized and newly successful. It can be and is being used to promote the range of savings and investments offered by NS&I to a public that is now more willing to listen. The important factor is the last aspect. Ensuring that the public continues to be all eyes and ears has to be the number one priority. And NS&I will achieve this by ensuring that it borrows the clothing of Premium Bonds and itself becomes the public byword for trust and integrity in a financial services market where there isn't as much as there was.

LOOKING FOR CLUES

Peter Bareau built the modern NS&I machine. Alan Cook ran it and made it successful. What will Jane Platt do? Acting Chief Executive, Trevor Bayley, who oversaw the role between Alan Cook and Jane Platt, said: "We have recognized that there is a need for NS&I to be more competitive in terms of products that are taxable."[5]

Jane Platt, with her long track record in financial services in the UK and internationally, took up her position in September 2006, just in time to witness the record monthly sales figures for Premium Bonds ahead of the 50th anniversary draw in December. And just in time to lead the successful completion of NS&I's current five year strategy (achieved in four years).

Just how is NS&I under Platt's control going to make sure that the Government continues to keep the National Debt as low as it possibly can be?

It's all summed up in the 2005/06 Annual Report. "To achieve Value Added, it's important that we give our customers a fair deal. And as we operate in a highly competitive market, we need to offer products that suit our customers' needs based on security, benefits and returns – backed by excellent service."

A NEW FIVE-YEAR STRATEGY FOR NS&I 2007–12

The prime objective is to deliver sustainable long-term value to stakeholders (government and customers) by simplifying, modernizing and diversifying the business:

- Growing the business at a steady rate.
- More concentration on added value to the taxpayer and customers.
- Maintaining an acceptable level of Net Financing and a loyal customer base.
- Building a low-cost business model to satisfy the long-term needs and expectations of customers.
- Diversifying the product range.

MORE APPEALING

The new strategy recognizes that previous strategies had centred on Premium Bonds and what a business risk this is. Very few organizations want to be a one product company.

With Premium Bonds as the flagship, NS&I now has the brand equity, the space, to develop and focus more attention on persuading people to buy other NS&I products. The plans are for NS&I to hold £91 billion of funds by 2012, featuring an expanded range of savings products, sold over the phone and the Internet, and partnership deals.

If raising awareness of existing products and creating new ones is the strategy, what tactics will NS&I use to make them more appealing to a market it thinks is just waiting to be appealed to? NS&I has already renamed the old-fashioned sounding Index Linked Savings Certificates to Inflation Beating Savings. More will follow.

BINGO LINGO

We're bombarded with money messages. Think money, think banks and banking products. As we know, the financial services industry uses a language all of its own. And, yes, it is very close to rocket science, which is where they like to keep it. Add a certain civil service mentality to the financial services industry, and we could all be wondering whether we speak the same tongue. So, what is "Value Added"? NS&I: "A measure of our cost-effectiveness in saving finance for Government. The total cost of raising funds is compared to how much it would cost the Government to raise funds through the wholesale market via gilts and Treasury Bills." [6] Any more questions?

To its credit, NS&I runs a financial jargon buster in the Helpful Information section of its website. And it is very good at explaining how it fits in between you and the Government.

DON'T BANK ON THE COMPETITORS

The future for NS&I depends on growing awareness and sales in a marketplace in which the competition from the top twenty banks and building societies is fierce. But NS&I has a headstart with excellent retention rates (86–88%) across all products in 2005/06. Trevor Bayley: "A real feat within the financial services industry."[7]

The future for NS&I may well depend on retaining its role as the antidote to other financial institutions, on giving a perfectly straight message that others do not give. And getting that message across with a human touch in settings that are not financially focused. NS&I has sponsored BBC Proms in the Park, the *Classic FM Morning Show,* The Classical BRIT Awards and show gardens at the Chelsea Flower Show. Unlike ERNIE's randomness, there's an observable pattern here. Red Nose Day, Big Brother and Glastonbury, it ain't. Mark Brooks: "NS&I has cornered the popular classical music arena." Indeed, NS&I used the 2006 Proms in the Park event to launch its publicity around the 50th anniversary and the five £1 million prizes.

Or on changing its tactics. Although NS&I has undoubtedly made its traditional deposit savings products more competitive, there are people who think that its products could be simpler overall. "Unfortunately, NS&I's range of products is fairly complicated and it can be difficult to choose the right one, particularly as many financial advisers are not prepared to help since they do not receive any commission." [8]

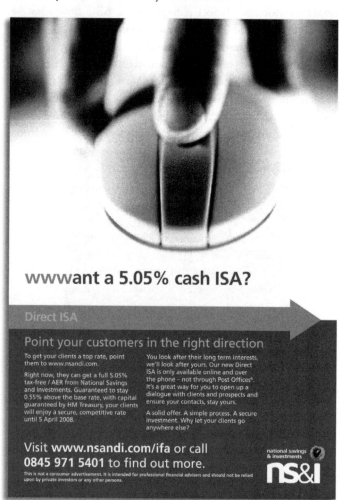

As I write, however, NS&I's tax-free Direct ISA is top of the market with an interest rate guaranteed to remain 0.55% above the base rate until at least 2008. How simple do people want it? Besides, NS&I knows that getting through to independent financial advisors (IFAs) is harder than with fee-based financial planners. But it's important that it does. And it is trying. IFAs recommend investments to the value of over £80 billion in the UK every year.[9] So, NS&I is focusing on those IFAs who are prepared to provide a more holistic approach to their clients' needs, rather than on individual products, allowing NS&I to be seen as the "rock solid foundation of any balanced portfolio."

One way or another, NS&I is trying to get you to change your attitude towards saving, by trying to meet your specific savings needs. The future is all about better products that are easier for you to understand, offer value for money, match the amount of risk you are willing to take while allowing you to see how your savings are doing as time passes.

NS&I has learned to operate in a society, in which we all now have a more ambivalent and relaxed attitude towards debt – by addressing people's concerns in relation to the way they live their lives: How much can I save if I am paying off my debts? How many different kinds of things am I saving for?

NS&I now tracks savings in the way that the Halifax and Nationwide record average house prices. Its *Quarterly Savings Survey* "aims to monitor trends in people's savings habits on a regular basis, at a national and regional level…and encourage the public to recognize the need to save and to save in a more strategic way, which is more suited to their individual needs in the short and long term."[10]

CAMELOTTERY

There is this sense among the Government, NS&I and Camelot that the National Lottery is not a competitor of Premium Bonds. This is not shared by the British media or the public.

Now Premium Bonds have raised their profile, the same is happening with the National Lottery. Camelot are keen to

153

announce partnership deals with Microsoft that will make the National Lottery more accessible to people via emerging channels. And nobody can say that Camelot has not learned from the way Premium Bonds has communicated its messages to the British public.

It, too, is putting values at the centre of its thinking as it makes its bid for the third National Lottery licence, due for renewal in 2009. This time it's linking with BSkyB, whose chief executive James Murdoch, said: "By integrating lottery services across Sky platforms – and in so doing harnessing the best in our multi-platform, interactive technologies – we hope to drive more value and fun into the whole lottery experience."[11]

Serious but fun, eh? Haven't we heard this somewhere before? Needless to say, with all this talk of interactivity and greater accessibility in the gambling world, everyone at NS&I should be watching attentively. Because, as far as I'm concerned, a more interactive National Lottery alongside easily accessible super-casinos would pose a great threat to Premium Bonds, NS&I and all forms of saving in this country.

AS FOR THE REST

Part of the future will certainly be how the Executive Agency called NS&I manages the often difficult relationship with the rest of the financial services industry. Considered to be in a privileged position, with government backing, NS&I can and must be seen to be doing the right thing by the public. As much as it may want to take advantage of all the bad publicity that follows any announcement from the top banks and building societies, it cannot do so overtly. For, it too, is part of the financial services industry, facing similar issues.

For example, a current hot media issue is the amount of assets sitting unclaimed in financial institutions that pay only lip service to returning them to the public. For NS&I, quietly letting the world know that it is far more proactive on dormant accounts than any high street bank will do the trick better than slapping it all over a billboard on Main Street.

In doing so, NS&I will have to watch that it does not get squeezed between the mainstream banking lobby and governmental political objectives around the resourcing of community initiatives like the mooted Social Investment Bank. The latter is not a direct threat to NS&I in terms of competition for resources. However, the idea came out of the Commission on Unclaimed Assets and there is no institution sitting on more of these than NS&I. Some people like to square the circle.

Anything could happen. And, successful though they currently are, NS&I and its flagship Premium Bonds cannot afford to be complacent. Executive Agency or no, NS&I may have to defend the integrity of its brand against pressure from commercial competitors on one side and the Government on the other. However, as we've seen, the best guard against this is to be different, offer something others can't, and above all, to maintain trust for another generation.

MORE TV?

Will this mean more TV for NS&I?

Maybe in the short term. But not the long term, if the words of Sir Alan Sugar are to be believed. "If I headed any of the commercial channels, what would worry me right now is the kind of device my own company makes, which is beginning to revolutionize the way we watch television in this country: the PVR, Personal Video Recorder... One of the main reasons I own a PVR is so I can skip adverts. I haven't watched an ad spot for over a year now – of course, apart from my own Premium Bonds one. Everybody is going to be doing the same soon. Digital devices make it easier than ever to programme out the ads, and what kind of brain-dead viewer is going to sit there solemnly watching them go through if they have the option of jumping? So in my view, advertising has had it, on television." [12]

It's hard to disagree with Sir Alan.

By the way, if you thought this was the reason you didn't see Sir Alan on TV promoting the 50th anniversary of the first draw in 2007, think again. His commitments with his TV programme, *The Apprentice*, unfortunately prevented him featuring in the latest NS&I TV advertising.

150 YEARS OF NATIONAL INVESTMENTS

To date, the advertising has been clear and effective. The NS&I website is simple and informative. The two 50th anniversaries have provided a great opportunity to publicize more £1 million prizes and boost sales.

But how does an understated brand that does not like to talk about itself continue to remain high in the public consciousness? Sir Alan Sugar won't be involved forever. The website will soon need to begin working a lot harder than it does now. Even Middle Britain expects more interactivity from financial websites.

Although the 150th NS&I anniversary in 2011 is looming, and the focus is likely to be more on the range of products other than Premium Bonds, there will still have to be some work done to keep the latter in the mind's eye. Following the recent years of great awareness-raising, there is now the opportunity to build closer and deeper relationships with customers. For a brand based on integrity, this, of course, needs to be done carefully.

What will we see? Maybe some tactical messages, encouraging people to put a little bit more by and keep a little bit more in, so increasing their chances of winning prizes. Perhaps some incentives to save a little more regularly?

What won't we see? ERNIE televised, surrounded by adjudicators. There will no flashing lights and analysis of the winning numbers. But there are ways of bringing people closer to a brand they have traditionally associated more with the Post Office than National Savings.

More and more people are buying online. There is an incredible hit-rate at the beginning of every month when people come online to check whether they have won. Eight hundred thousand people a month are in and out like a ferret in a drainpipe and NS&I does very little to keep them there.

Not many brands get such an opportunity to have a deeper conversation with their customers. NS&I need to look into ways of doing this without compromising the brand values, i.e. don't become too populist (we've got the National Lottery for that), retain the correct amount of aloofness for the times. Indeed, in doing what it does with a human touch, there is still something to aspire to as it notches up a century and a half of public service.

SAVING AND PROSPERING

A VERY BRITISH INSTITUTION

In 2003, the "Britain's Best-Kept Secret" campaign asserted that Premium Bonds were part of the *financial* fabric of the nation. They are more than that. They are part of the *essential* fabric of the nation.

There is something about Premium Bonds that says "there are still values and this is what is good about this country." And this type of thinking probably applies to the vast majority of Premium Bond Holders with less than £1,000 worth of Premium Bonds, rather than the "financially capable" who are relatively well off and money focused.

The type of thinking that started Premium Bonds in the 1950s was aimed at people who had very little. It was an encouragement to think of the future, at a time when the country was beginning to show signs of prosperity after years of austerity and wartime hardship. And there is still something of this attitude in Premium Bonds. They do represent a continuation of values that are the antithesis of a live-fast, throwaway, credit-based culture. Premium Bonds have thrift at their heart.

Yes, there are many people who have forgotten about the Premium Bonds they hold. There are many who are in "Premium Bondage." Some are passive. But, even though there are other and better places to put your money in terms of returns, there are just as many people for whom Premium Bonds reflect a willingness and determination to retain a certain set of British values.

If you fell asleep in 1956 and woke up in 2006 in front of a blaring TV to a culture that looks like a relentless chav-lebrity karaoke peepshow, would you still find that same underlying sense of Britishness? Yes, I think you would. It's buried, but it's there.

AN EMOTIONAL FUND

For the money-minded, however, Premium Bonds are currently a very rational investment choice. Especially when they have £30,000 to invest and have already maximized all their tax-avoiding activities, from ISAs to offshoring.

But investment in any product represents a sum made up of the rational and the irrational. Or the tangible and intangible. Or the pragmatic and emotional. The share of these two conflicting and yet complementary factors is different in every individual, every time, with every brand. This is what is fascinating about any brand. Why should Premium Bonds be different?

One thing's for sure, for most people the emotional fund they invest in a brand has very little to do with what it is worth in a rational sense. A brand is only worth it *because* of these emotional values, not in spite of them. I am attached to my football club, even though, rationally, they are from top to bottom a morally redundant bunch of no-hopers who do not deserve my support. It goes beyond any rational thinking. And no matter how good or attractive *your* football team is, I will always hate them. Never mind the replica shirts, I have invested emotionally in this football club brand over many, many years. It's too late to change now.

The big question is, are we really as attached to the financial brands we buy as much as we are to our football team? The answer is obviously no, but the difference is one of extreme not of kind. A brand is a brand.

Cynics may point out that the reason people stay with brands so long is because they're too lazy to move on. In the case of financial brands, they may not be sufficiently motivated to do themselves the favour of putting their money where it will really protect their future. So, in your passivity, you are effectively gambling with your future.

When you invest in a brand, however, the very last thing you are doing is gambling. You are doing the very opposite. You are actually re-investing in your sense of self, your own identity.

THE BEST OF THE OLD AND THE NEW

So much for personal identity. What about collective identity? By representing our collective identity in a very quiet way, Premium Bonds have become a very wily brand. Their brand values are steeped in tradition and an old sense of Britishness, yet their brand strategy is focused on a new sense of Britishness that has hardly begun to manifest – less a sense of community, and more an appeal to an individual savviness and cleverness with money that is so, well, un-British, without ever being silly or irresponsible.

Sir Alan Sugar managed to personify both sets of values – the old and the new. Their entire future success will depend on how Premium Bonds manage to carry both sets of values into relevant messages to the public.

And yet, I really believe that, in the case of Premium Bonds, you are associating your identity with the innate sense of security that lies underneath what it is to be British. Everything in moderation. We have centuries of it. And call us what it will, the rest of the world respects us for it and yearns for it. So what if we don't know the words to our own national anthem! So what if we're crap at sports and the whole world enjoys beating us at games we invented! What the little Englanders, Europhobes and insecure nationalists among us fail to realize, when they prey upon our worries and fears, is that British identity is neither being lost, nor does it need to be overly protected. Yes, it's buffeted by an aggressive, self-centred media, but it's right here, rolling with the changes, assimilating all and everything that the world throws at it. (Cue the music: "Land of Hope and Glory.")

When this country was picking itself up from its knees in the 1950s, a very different government realized that people needed some guidance on the future, to recreate that ancient stability for upcoming generations. Thus was the creation of Premium Bonds an affirmation of British values, a re-assertion of what had made this nation successful for centuries. No wonder it's deeply embedded in the national psyche.

Kick and rebel against it all you want and put your money somewhere else if you insist, but Premium Bonds are here to stay. They know what they stand for. They are the place, or a place, where we place our sense of survival and continuity, our faith in stable government (even if you don't like the Government in power).

Fifty years ago Premium Bonds were new, but they are now part of our national foundation that the baby boomers of the late 40s, 50s and 60s have grown up with. We are saving for ourselves in a way that enables us to save for our country. We may not exactly know where the money goes but there is something especially British about Premium Bonds that is close to our hearts today. A national treasure for the 21st century.

2020: SUPERUNCERTAINTY

Yet this is a century that has started with great collective and personal insecurity. When we look into this future we tend to bring it far closer than it actually turns out to be. We expect to see the product of our current thinking in our own lifetimes. Me? I expect to be able to fulfil my dream of orbiting the planet by the time I'm picking up my pension.

Back in the late 1950s, when Premium Bonds were introduced, life was picking up a bit of pace. The space race was on. When the Americans landed on the Moon in the late 1960s,

TV programmes and films like *Star Trek, Space 1999* and *2001: A Space Odyssey*, suggested we'd be living there and beyond, very shortly. If that happens at all this 21st century, then it will be the Chinese and not the Americans who achieve it.

Back in 1982, the film *Bladerunner* depicted a savage, bleak, poly-racial, dystopian world of Los Angeles in November 2019, featuring replicants from Earth's "off-world colonies." Fortunately, this is clearly not going to happen in this timeframe (off-shoring, yes, but off-world colonies, no). But by 2018, will Britain be hosting the World Cup? It's not that far off, you know.

But as politicians, scientists and campaigners try to focus our minds on a three degree rise in global average temperatures by the year 2100, we remain more concerned about whether the postman will deliver that cheque next month because life is uncertain enough today without tomorrow's worries.

HAVING AND HOLDING

Still, we dream on. When we think of the future, we think less about saving and more about winning.

Like pop music, our generation didn't invent it. Fifty years ago the big "winning" story of the time was Premium Bonds. Today, it's super-casinos. Just because the UK government is licensing super-casinos and making gambling that much easier, does not mean that, by 2020, we'll be a nation of addicts, unable to decide whether to live in a virtual or real world.

In this world of super-uncertainty, however, a brand like Premium Bonds can only prosper as long as it remains visible. As with the arrival of the National Lottery, the inevitable advent of super-casinos will benefit Premium Bonds. The sheer publicity, negative or otherwise, will remind people what they have and hold and would like to continue having and holding. For them, Premium Bonds will forever be a flutter with your money back.

The Premium Bonds brand will need to monitor developments in the gambling world. It will never be glitzy, with bells and whistles, but it will need to be not too far behind – in terms of technology, information flow and whatever it takes to satisfy the growing appetite of the individual in a world of insecurity.

As long as it remembers how relevant it is and needs to be, taps into the way people's minds are changing now and satisfies these demands. If Premium Bonds continue to succeed, it will be because they continue to be the alternative to whatever's latest. They just need to stay in touch. And keep a human touch.

WHAT A CARRY ON!

I've been trying to touch this brand called Premium Bonds for months now. I've shaken hands with Agent Million and interfaced with ERNIE himself.

For me, Premium Bonds are no ordinary brand. It's very clear, however, that in the ways it operates as a business and communicates its message to the world, the Premium Bonds brand cannot be surreal or fantastic. Yet I find that most of my thinking about it is surreal and fantastic.

We're covering half a century of recent history, yet here's a brand which has hardly appeared in it, save for the beginning and its 50th anniversary. This contemporary of Queen Elizabeth, this survivor. A brand fronted by a chaotic robot with a big personality and a body that shrinks in size every 16 years.

The simplicity of the product and the audacity of the numbers involved – customers, bonds, pounds sterling – are mind-boggling. The brand that is its own Mythsonian Institute. The lure of the million pound prize, despite the winning odds of one person in three planet Earth populations.

Then there's the whole reason for the existence of Premium Bonds – ostensibly, to encourage the nation to save from the 1950s onwards, yet also a means of contributing to paying off the National Debt – that intangible figure on a balance sheet that nobody ever talks about.

A "squalid raffle" that ends up involving over 38% of the population, massively over-exceeding the expectations of its creators and its current inheritors. A brand that is so successful that it has to be careful not to be seen to be too successful.

Overall, the sheer greyness and solidity of it all, down to people saying it would be impossible to write a book about Premium Bonds, because there is just nothing to say. In case you haven't noticed, I simply do not see it that way.

This secret, this ever-so-hidden brand that is within us and all around us – literally and metaphorically – is a national treasure. It's absurd. And, of course, it's surreal!

I get a warm feeling from Premium Bonds. All the way from gawky Norman Wisdom's promotional support in the early days to the deep, frowning lines of seriousness on Sir Alan Sugar's forehead today. They make me smile. And, now that I know what I know, Premium Bonds will be making me smile in 2020. Nice one, ERNIE!

Happy 50th Birthday Ernie!

Notes

1 *Consumer Attitudes to Saving – UK*, Mintel Report, February 2005.

2 *Financial capability in the UK: Delivering change*, FSA, 2004.

3 *Closing the Savings Gap – Why the Savings Industry Wants Change*, Association of British Insurers, July 2002.

4 Daniel Farey-Jones, "EuroDirect lands huge database commission from National Savings," Brand Republic, 17th March 2005.

5 Phillip Inman, "Sugar helps sweeten Premium Bond coffers by £8bn," Guardian, 21st July 2006.

6 *NS&I Report and Accounts*, 2005/06.

7 ibid.

8 "Has National Savings changed its payout policy?," Guardian Unlimited, 30th November 2006.

9 *NS&I Report and Accounts*, 2005/06.

10 www.nsandi.com

11 Mark Banham, "Camelot set to partner with Sky for interactive lottery," Brand Republic, 9th February 2007.

12 Dick Emery & Mary Collins, *The Next Big Thing: A collection of essays, musings and rants on the future of British broadcasting,* Premium Publishing, 2005.

APPENDIX
PREMIUM BONDS – A TIMELINE FOR MIDDLE BRITAIN

What follows is a socio-cultural-economic timeline for Premium Bonds against the background of saving and gambling. Wherever you find yourself within it, be sure that Premium Bonds are never far behind.

1568
The first English lottery. The Great Elizabethan or Queen's Lottery is not a success.

1612
A state-sponsored lottery is raised for the colonization of Virginia.

1709
An Act of Parliament suppresses lotteries, effectively bringing them under state control.

1737
The first of five annual state-sponsored lotteries to pay for Westminster Bridge.

1753
A state-sponsored lottery establishes the British Museum.

1776
State-run lotteries are now an annual event during the reign of George III.

1807
After abolishing the slave trade, William Wilberforce and Henry Thornton commit to abolishing lotteries.

MP Samuel Whitbread fails to get Parliament to accept his idea of a Savings Bank run by the Post Office®.

1810
One of the most successful early Savings Banks is set up in Ruthwell, Dumfries.

1817
The first Savings Bank Act regulates Savings Banks, requiring them to invest in government stock.

1826

In law, the state lottery is abolished. 18 October sees the running of the last state lottery for 168 years.

1854

During the Crimean War, British servicemen have sent over £100,000 back to families in Britain.

1860

Queen Victoria issues a proclamation supporting the suppression of all public gaming houses.

1861

William Gladstone's Post Office Savings Bank Act establishes National Savings, offering a "depositor's book" – the original Ordinary Account, at 301 Post Offices in areas where existing Trustee Savings Banks are scarce.

1880

Postmaster General, Henry Fawcett, introduces deposit cards to which twelve penny postage stamps can be attached, to save the minimum deposit of one shilling. In six months, half a million cards are filled up.

1893

In his *History of National Lotteries*, J Ashton says that state lotteries have "developed into a voluntary taxation appealing to the national taste for gambling, and fostered by the Government, in order to help out the annual supplies."

1915

William Heath Robinson, cartoonist and illustrator, famous for drawings of eccentric machines, produces large numbers of cartoons depicting ever-more-unlikely secret weapons being used in the First World War.

1916

The National War Savings Committee is introduced to help the war effort. Premium Bonds are first proposed at a National Savings committee meeting, but are rejected by Chancellor Reginald McKenna.

1918

Five million people in 1,840 War Savings committees and 41,301 War Savings Associations, and 6,000 Agents working through 14,000 establishments, have raised £217m during the First World War. Special savings stamps are introduced. The Savings Department produces Britannia's head stamps. The National Savings Committee has a swastika stamp – a Sanskrit symbol for good fortune.

1923

Littlewoods Football Pools is founded.

1933

With the advent of Hitler, the swastika stamp is dropped. The Post Office, Trustee Savings Banks and National Savings Committee reach agreement on a common savings stamp.

The Royal Commission on Lotteries and Betting comments that "lotteries take their place among the expedients which are resorted to when other and more reputable methods of finance have failed."

1934

The Betting and Lotteries Act legalizes lotteries again, but under strict conditions.

1943

A machine used by British code breakers to solve messages at Bletchley Park during the Second World War is nicknamed Heath Robinson, in honour of the famous cartoonist.

1940

Winston Churchill becomes British Prime Minister.

1944

Colossus – the world's first programmable digital electronic computer – comes into service at Bletchley Park, moving code breaking to a higher level.

1945

Twelve million people in over 270,000 National Savings Groups have saved over £1.75bn in over 20 million accounts.

The post-war British public returns a Labour government led by Clement Attlee.

Food rationing becomes stricter than ever and now includes bread.

1946

The beginning of the baby-boom generation.

Football Pools companies launch the Treble Chance, with a single large jackpot.

1947

Bell Laboratories builds the first practical transistor – the future of electronics and computers.

First of the celebrated post-war Ealing Comedies, *Hue and Cry*, starring Alastair Sim.

PREMIUM BONDS

1949

Several successful Ealing Comedies embed a sense of post-war British culture: *Whisky Galore!* and *Passport to Pimlico*. In *Kind Hearts and Coronets*, Alec Guinness plays eight different characters.

1950

A 65-year-old man can expect to live another 12 years, until 77; a woman has another 14 years, until 79.

Alan Turing introduces the Turing test, to test a machine's capability to perform human-like conversation.

1951

The Royal Commission on Betting, Lotteries and Gaming says that a national lottery would lead to an increase in the volume of gambling, so the state should not provide any form of gambling facility.

Winston Churchill becomes British Prime Minister for the second time.

The famous Festival of Britain attempts to give Britons a feeling of recovery and progress.

Award-winning Ealing Comedy, *The Lavender Hill Mob*, starring Alec Guinness and Stanley Holloway.

The Goon Show and *Life with the Lyons* debut on BBC Radio.

1952

The accession of Queen Elizabeth II.

1953

Norman Wisdom's famous "gump" character debuts in the film *Trouble in Store*.

Sugar is no longer rationed.

The famous Stanley Matthews Cup Final: Blackpool come from behind to beat Bolton Wanderers 4–3.

1954

Yes, we have some bananas! The end of all food rationing in the UK.

The world's first transistor radio, the Regency TR-1, costs $49.95 in the US (equivalent to $525 today).

Roger Bannister becomes the first man to run the mile in less than 4 minutes.

Debut of radio comedy series, *Hancock's Half Hour*, starring Tony Hancock, Kenneth Williams, Sid James, Hattie Jacques.

Morecambe and Wise debut and flop on BBC TV in their first show, *Running Wild*.

1955
Sir Anthony Eden becomes Prime Minister, with Harold Macmillan as his Chancellor.

The launch of ITV.

A TV licence costs £4 and television is only transmitted for eight hours each day, not before 9am or after 11pm. There is no TV between 6pm and 7pm so that children can be put to bed.

Hughie Green, host of radio's talent show, *Opportunity Knocks*, hosts *Double Your Money* on ITV.

The arrival of Elvis Presley and the beginning of the pop era.

1956
Chancellor Harold Macmillan introduces Premium Savings Bonds in his annual budget. He launches Series "A" Premium Savings Bonds on 1st November in Trafalgar Square. Premium Savings Bonds go on sale at 33,000 Post Offices, banks and trustee savings banks, National Savings clubs and employee schemes in 3,800 companies. Premium Bonds achieve £5m of sales in the first day and £54m by the end of the year. Bonds become eligible after they've been held for six months. Maximum holding is £500.

Lytham St Annes becomes the home of Premium Bonds.

The Wolfenden Report recommends the legalization of homosexuality.

"Lay Down Your Arms" by Anne Shelton is number 1 in the UK pop charts, reflecting the Suez Crisis.

John McCarthy coins the term "Artificial Intelligence" to describe the making of Intelligent machines.

John Osborne's play, *Look Back in Anger*, spawns a flurry of "angry young men" films.

British Rail renames "Third Class" passenger facilities as "Second Class." Second Class facilities had been abolished in 1875, leaving just First Class and Third Class.

1957

Harold Macmillan becomes Prime Minister.

On 1st June, broadcast live on radio and TV, ERNIE is started by Postmaster General, Ernest Marples, and runs the first Premium Bonds draw featuring 49 million Premium Bonds. The Premium Bond Prize fund rate is 4.0%. The odds of winning a prize in the first draw are 2,095–1. Top prize is £1,000.

"Pretty Butterfly" by Andy Williams, is number 1 in the UK pop charts.

Pye UK develop and market the first transistor radio in Britain.

The Clitheroe Kid debuts on BBC Radio.

1958

There are 10 million Premium Bonds holders and the maximum holding is raised from £500 to £800.

The first Miss Premium Bonds competition takes place on the Civil Service Sports and Social Club annual fete day in Lytham St Annes. It is won by Marny Birchall, whose job is to tour the country supporting promotions.

The first *Carry On* film, *Carry On Sergeant*, starring Kenneth Williams, Charles Hawtrey, Hattie Jacques, Kenneth Connor, Terry Scott, Bob Monkhouse, Shirley Eaton, Bill Owen and Dora Bryan.

Bruce Forsyth compères *Sunday Night at the London Palladium*.

1959

Birth of the author of *Nice Little ERNIE: A 21st century national treasure*.

Frederik Pohl and Cyril M Kornbluth's *Wolfbane*, a story in which a rogue planet, populated by strange machines known as Pyramids, uses humans as components in a huge computer.

Cliff Richard's "Living Doll" peaks at number 1 in the UK pop charts for six summer weeks.

1960

The top Premium Bonds prize goes up from £1,000 to £5,000. Series "B" Bonds are launched. The Premium Bond Prize fund rate is 4.0%. The chances of winning a prize are 9,600–1.

Harold Macmillan's government legalizes betting shops.

The first *Beyond The Fringe* shows, featuring Peter Cook and Dudley Moore.

Penguin Books wins the *Lady Chatterley's Lover* obscenity trial. Chief prosecutor, Mervyn Griffith-Jones, had asked if it were the kind of book "you would wish your wife or servants to read."

The film *Saturday Night, Sunday Morning* is the first of the social realist or "kitchen sink" dramas.

1961

The one millionth Premium Bond prize. Thirteen million people have invested £339m. The average holding is £26.

Viv "spend, spend, spend" Nicholson wins £151,000 on the Football Pools (equivalent to £3m today).

BAFTA award-winning *A Taste of Honey*, starring Dora Bryan, reveals more northern working class life.

1962

Judi Dench and Bob Hope promote Premium Bonds around the 5th birthday.

First series of TV sitcom, *Steptoe & Son*, the nation's favourite rag and bone men.

A Kind of Loving and *The Loneliness of the Long Distance Runner* are the latest gritty social realist films.

Satirical TV comedy show *That Was The Week That Was* lampoons Postmaster General, Reginald Bevins, who threatens "to do something about it."

1963

Bruce Forsyth promotes Premium Bonds around the 6th birthday.

Sixteen-year-old Alan Sugar sells car aerials and electrical goods out of a van bought with his savings of £100.

The downfall of Harold Macmillan's government, heavily implicated by the Profumo Sex Scandal.

Another northern realism film, *Billy Liar*, features Tom Courtenay and Julie Christie.

The Beatles release their first record, "Twist and Shout."

The Dick Emery Show debuts on TV. "Ooh, you are awful…but I like you!"

First *Doctor Who* TV series.

1964

The maximum Premium Bond holding is raised from £800 to £1,000. The Prize Fund Rate is still 4.0%. And the chances of winning a prize are still 9,600–1.

Harold Wilson's Labour government wins the General Election.

The first Beatles film, "A Hard Day's Night."

TV comedy series debut of *The Likely Lads*.

1966

The introduction of a quarterly top Premium Bond prize of £25,000, up from £5,000. The average holding is £38. The total Premium Bond investment is now £575m. The Prize Fund Rate is still 4.0%. The chances of winning a prize are 9,600–1.

Harold Wilson's Labour government is returned for a second term.

The England football team wins the World Cup.

Alf Garnett becomes a national favourite in TV sitcom, *Till Death Us Do Part*.

1967

The maximum Premium Bond holding is raised from £1,000 to £1,250. The Prize Fund Rate is still 4.0%. The chances of winning a prize are still 9,600–1.

The Post Office Savings Bank opens an office in Durham and launches its first TV advertising.

The Sexual Offences Act decriminalizes homosexual activity between consenting adults, 21 and over.

Judi Dench wins a BAFTA television award for Best Actress in *Talking to a Stranger*.

Bob Monkhouse hosts *The Golden Shot* gameshow.

1968

The Prize Fund Rate goes up to 4.625%. The total investment is now £692m. The chances of winning a prize are still 9,600–1.

Alan Sugar founds the electronics and computer company Amstrad.

Frankie Howerd stars in *Carry On Doctor.*

Enoch Powell makes his infamous "rivers of blood" speech.

Mike Yarwood, debuts on TV with *Will the Real Mike Yarwood Stand Up?* "I mean that most sincerely, folks."

First appearance of *Dad's Army* and Father, *Dear Father* TV sitcoms.

The sinister HAL 9000 (Heuristically Programmed Algorithmic) computer, stars in Stanley Kubrick's *2001: A Space Odyssey.* "Dave...you are destroying my mind."

1969

The Post Office becomes a public corporation and the Department for National Savings splits from the Post Office to become one of the largest government departments, now responsible to Treasury ministers.

Tony Jacklin wins the British Open Golf Championship, the first Briton to do so for 18 years.

TV debuts for Monty Python's *Flying Circus, On The Buses* and *The Benny Hill Show.*

The first ATM is launched and people have easier access to cash without stepping into a bank.

The average annual UK salary is £1,760 and the average UK house price is £4,640.

1970
The Beatles split.

Frankie Howerd stars in TV sitcom, *Up Pompeii.* "Titter ye not!"

1971
The biggest Premium Bonds prize doubles from £25,000 to £50,000. The maximum Premium Bond holding is raised from £1,250 to £2,000. The average holding is £46. The UK inflation rate is running at 10.3%. The total investment is now up to £889m. The Prize Fund Rate is still 4.625%. The chances of winning a prize are now down to 10,400–1.

First TV airing of *The Two Ronnies* and Bruce Forsyth's *Generation Game.*

1972
Twenty million Premium Bond holders have £962m invested. The minimum purchase is now £2.

ERNIE is mentioned in a song on the album *Thick as a Brick* by UK rock band, Jethro Tull.

Debut of TV sitcoms, *Are You Being Served?* and *Love Thy Neighbour.*

1973
ERNIE 2 is introduced to cope with 10-digit serial numbers as total investments reach £1bn. Twenty-five prizes of £1,000 are introduced into the weekly prize draws. The UK inflation rate is running at 9.4%. The Prize Fund rate is now up to 4.875%. The chances of winning a prize are now improved to 10,200–1.

The Page Committee to review National Savings recommends the winding up of the voluntary National Savings movement and that Trustee Savings Banks be freed from governmental control.

TV debut of *Last Of The Summer Wine* and *Some Mothers Do 'Ave 'Em.* Character Frank Spencer's mother sends Christmas cards to ERNIE, in the hope that he will favour her Premium Bonds.

PREMIUM BONDS

1974

The top monthly Premium Bonds jackpot rises from £50,000 to £75,000, promoted by Frankie Howerd.

A single monthly prize of £25,000 is introduced. The weekly £25,000 prize is raised to £50,000. The £250 prize is withdrawn. The UK inflation rate is running at 17.1%. The total investment in Premium Bonds is up to £1.04bn. The Prize Fund Rate is up to 5.5%. The chances of winning a prize are now down again to 10,500–1.

The Government is forced to introduce the Three Day Week, in an attempt to conserve electricity, which is in short supply due to industrial action by coal miners.

The year sees a hung Parliament, as Labour takes over from the Conservative government, following years of industrial strife. Six months later, Labour wins a narrow overall majority.

First airing of TV sitcoms, *Rising Damp, It Ain't Half Hot Mum* and *Porridge.*

1975

Over 100,000 Premium Bond prizes per month are given out by ERNIE. The UK inflation rate peaks at 26.9%. The total investment is up to £1.1bn and the Prize Fund Rate is still 5.5%. The chances of winning a prize are still 10,500–1.

Premium Bonds and other National Savings products are transferred to a new site at Marton in Blackpool.

National Savings introduces Index-Linked Savings Certificates.

First series of TV sitcom, *Fawlty Towers* and *The Good Life*.

John Hurt wins best actor BAFTA for his portrayal of gay icon, Quentin Crisp, in *The Naked Civil Servant.*

1976

Premium Bonds Holder numbers are introduced to make it easier for customers to check their holdings. The Premium Bonds jackpot rises from £75,000 to £100,000. The minimum purchase rises from £2 to £5. The average holding is £56.

The UK inflation rate is running at 15.0%. The total Premium Bond investment is now £1.18bn. The Prize Fund Rate moves up to 5.625%. The chances of winning a prize are now down again to 10,800–1.

National Savings stamps are withdrawn from sale and the Trustee Savings Bank becomes independent.

ROGER MOORE, AKA JAMES BOND, PROMOTES PREMIUM BONDS.

First TV series of sitcoms, *The Fall and Rise of Reginald Perrin* and *Open All Hours*. And *George and Mildred*.

1977

Queen Elizabeth II's Silver Jubilee is celebrated around the nation.

The year sees the biggest leap in numbers of Premium Bond Holders, from 22 to 25 million.

The quick rise and fall of the Punk Rock phenomenon, led by the Sex Pistols and their "number 1" record, "God Save the Queen."

Virginia Wade wins Wimbledon.

The debut of K9, the Doctor's robotic dog, in *Doctor Who*. "Affirmative, Master!" *The Morecambe and Wise Christmas Show* attracts 28 million viewers, still a UK TV record for a single light entertainment broadcast. Debut of *Citizen Smith*.

R2-D2 and C-3PO become very popular robots with human characteristics in the first Star Wars film.

1978

Premium Bonds celebrate their 21st birthday with a reception at Manchester Town Hall. National Savings produces a booklet, 20 Questions on Ernie, with a picture of ERNIE on the cover with a mini-skirted blonde sitting on his lap.

The maximum Premium Bond holding is raised from £2,000 to £3,000.

The National Savings Committee winds up after 62 years.

Lord Rothschild's Royal Commission recommends the setting up of a national lottery, arguing that it is not wrong for the State to promote gambling that is socially harmless and raises money for good causes.

Britain's "Winter of Discontent." The Labour government tries to keep pay rises below 5%. Public service workers strike. Rubbish rots uncollected on the streets and the army puts out fires in Green Goddesses.

German electronic band, Kraftwerk, release their seminal work, "The Man-Machine."

First appearance of Marvin, The Paranoid Android, in the radio version of *The Hitchhiker's Guide to the Galaxy*.

1979

National Savings workers go on strike, causing chaos with the running of Premium Bonds.

Margaret Thatcher becomes the UK's first female Prime Minister. UK inflation rises to 15.6%, the highest for two years.

To deal with administrative chaos on Premium Bonds, National Savings drastically cuts the number of prizes available, from 128,000 to 30,000, temporarily withdrawing the lowest level £25 and £50 prizes, reducing the chances of winning by four times, down to a massive 44,000 to1, the longest odds ever. As a result, cumulative Premium Bond sales go down for the first time. In August, September, October and December, more people are cashing in than are buying.

The first series of *To the Manor Born, Terry and June* and *Not the Nine O'Clock News.*

1980

In January, National Savings introduces a new prize structure. £50 is now the lowest value prize. There's now a new monthly prize of £100,000. The Premium Bond selling trend continues. In February and March, more people sell than buy.

In response, the maximum Premium Bonds holding rises from £2,000 to £10,000. The Premium Bonds jackpot rises from £100,000 to a whopping £250,000. The top prize winners are now informed in person.

The UK inflation rate is running at 21.8%. The Prize Fund Rate is increased to 7.0%. Total investment in Premium Bonds has moved up to £1.44bn. The number of prizes are up to 70,000 a month, roughly what they were in 1970 and the chances of winning are shorter at 18,000 to 1, twice as long as in 1970.

For the first time, the Government sets the Department for National Savings a specific target for its share of funding central government borrowing through national savings.

PREMIUM BONDS

The pop band Madness features the song "E.R.N.I.E." on *Absolutely*, their second album.

Prime Minister, Margaret Thatcher makes her famous announcement that "the lady's not for turning." She removes the link between state pensions and earnings. Pensions now go up each year in relation to prices.

The first TV series of *Hi-de-Hi* and *Yes, Minister.*

Ex-Beatle, John Lennon, is murdered in New York.

1981
UK inflation averages 11.9% for the year and the country is in recession. The total Premium Bond investment is £1.49bn. The number of customers holding an average of £59 is 25.4 million. The Prize Fund rate is 7.0%. With 100,000 monthly prizes, the chances of winning are better again, at 15,500–1.

The launch of the IBM Personal Computer revolutionizes the computer market.

First airing of TV sitcom, *Only Fools and Horses*.

1982
The number of Premium Bond Holders peaks at 26 million, a figure which it has yet to reach again.

Margaret Thatcher wins a second General Election on the back of victory in The Falklands War.

Ridley Scott's *Bladerunner* predicts a dystopian world of out-of-control androids in 2019.

The Boys from the Blackstuff TV series, a tragic view of how recession affects ordinary working people in Liverpool.

Debut for TV comedy shows *Alas Smith and Jones, Wood and Walters* and *The Young Ones.*

1983
The Department for National Savings introduces a new logo.

First-ever series of *Blackadder* and *Auf Wiedersehen, Pet.*

1984
At 152,000, the amount of monthly Premium Bond prizes dispensed is now back to 1979 levels. The £2,000 Bond denomination is introduced.

The beginning of the Miners' Strike.

First series of the satirical puppet show, *Spitting Image.*

1985

The minimum Premium Bond purchase rises from £5 to £10. UK inflation is slightly up, averaging around 6%. The Prize Fund Rate is the highest it's ever been at 7.75%. Total funds invested go up to £1.8bn. The odds of winning are better than they have been since 1979, at 11,000–1.

The Government funding target for the Department of National Savings is removed.

1986

The total Premium Bond investment goes up to £1.89bn. Down for the first time, 24.6 million customers have an average holding of £77. The UK inflation rate cools to an average 3.4% for the year and the Premium Bond Prize Fund rate stays at 7.75%. The chances of winning are still good, at 11,000–1.

The Government introduces portable personal pensions.

First appearance of TV sitcom, *Bread*. And *Naked Video,* launching Glaswegian ne'er do well, Rab C Nesbitt.

1987

A new Premium Bonds prize structure reduces the number of middle range prizes and increases the number of £50 prizes.

The Conservatives win a third consecutive term.

The last ever Miss Premium Bonds competition takes place.

1988

With 2.2 billion Premium Bonds in circulation, ERNIE 3 is introduced by TV personality and popular scientist, Professor Heinz Wolff, to speed up the draw.

1989

The minimum Premium Bonds purchase level for savers over 16 is raised to £100. The UK inflation rate is running at 8.2%. The total investment in Premium Bonds reaches £2.33bn and the Prize Fund Rate is 6.5%. But November sees the first deficit sales month for 9 years.

First Direct, part of Midland Bank, is the UK's first telephone-banking service.

Creature Comforts wins an Oscar. *A Grand Day* Out introduces Wallace & Gromit and wins a BAFTA.

1990

Recession. Inflation hits 10.9%. Total investment dips to £2.32bn, with only three positive Premium Bond sales months. The Prize Fund Rate is 6.5% and the chances of winning a prize are still 11,000–1.

The Poll Tax riots in London.

Tim Berners-Lee and Robert Cailliau create the World Wide Web, a system of interlinked, hypertext documents that runs over the Internet, a collection of interconnected computer networks.

First TV appearance of Hyacinth Bucket in *Keeping Up Appearances*. And Victor Meldrew in *One Foot in the Grave*.

Margaret Thatcher is replaced by John Major.

The first TV series of *Have I Got News For You, Vic Reeves' Big Night Out, Drop the Dead Donkey* and *The Harry* "loads-a-money" *Enfield Show.*

1991

The total Premium Bond investment is now £2.38bn. The average holding is £101. The country remains in recession. The UK inflation rate averages 5.9% for the year. The Prize Fund rate is 6.5%. Winners of £50 prizes can now re-invest them into Premium Bonds.

Alan Sugar becomes chairman of Tottenham Hotspur FC.

1992

Winners of £100 prizes can now re-invest them into Premium Bonds.

Every country in the EC has a national lottery except the UK. State lotteries are held in 116 countries around the world. The UK government advocates a single national lottery to raise money for good causes.

Voters return John Major's Conservative Party.

Black Wednesday. Chancellor Norman Lamont is forced to withdraw the Pound from the European Exchange Rate Mechanism. The Bank rate jumps from 10% to 15%.

The Premium Bond Prize Fund rate remains at 6.5%.

TV debuts for *The Jack Dee Show, Absolutely Fabulous* and *Men Behaving Badly.*

1993

The minimum Premium Bonds purchase for all savers is now £100 and the £5,000 denomination is introduced. The maximum holding doubles from £10,000 to £20,000. This leads to a buying rush, with National Savings recording the highest ever monthly total for Premium Bond sales.

The inflation rate is 1.3% and the Prize Fund rate is 5.0%. With 23 million people now holding £3bn in investment, the odds on winning a prize rise to 15,000–1, the highest since the 1991 recession.

The 1993 National Lottery Act defines five good causes to which 28% of revenues will be directed: the arts; sport; national heritage; Millennium projects; charities.

Wallace and Gromit's *The Wrong Trousers* wins an Oscar.

1994

The Premium Bonds jackpot is raised to £1m, eligibility for the draw falls from three months to one and all weekly prizes are withdrawn. £230m is invested in Premium Bonds in the first month, more than double the previous month's figure. Monthly sales break the £100m barrier.

The first Premium Bonds millionaire lives in Surrey and holds £10,000 worth of Bonds. The winning Bond is one of £2,000 bought just 10 months before the draw.

November sees the introduction of the National Lottery, run by Camelot and launched by Noel Edmonds.

The Vicar Of Dibley TV sitcom reflects a change in law that allows the ordination of female vicars.

1995

Total investments in Premium Bonds now amount to over £5bn and the 50 millionth prize is awarded. Customers can now automatically re-invest their prizes. Premium Bonds are no longer on sale in banks and building societies – they have their own competing products.

A MIntel study shows that the National Lottery has encouraged 17% of the public to participate in further forms of gambling. Gamblers Anonymous receives an increase of 17% in the number of calls it receives.

Assistant editor of the *Daily Telegraph*, Boris Johnson, calls the National Lottery a "tax on the stupid."

1996

Peter Bareau joins National Savings as Chief Executive. National Savings finally becomes an Executive Agency – of the Chancellor of the Exchequer.

UK inflation is low again at 2.4% and the Prize Fund rate a reasonable 4.75%. Premium Bonds can now be bought over the telephone. Sales rocket again, with two new monthly records of £253m in January and £274m in October.

Total Premium Bond investment passes £7bn. The average holding is £331. The amount of monthly prizes is fixed at 350,000. The odds of winning are no longer fixed and move steadily out from 18,000–1 to 23,000–1.

Statisticians reckon that you need to have £13m to live the life of a true millionaire.

PREMIUM BONDS

1997

Premium Bonds celebrate their 40th anniversary by sponsoring the Celebrity Theatre at BBC Gardener's World Live at the NEC in Birmingham.

July sees record monthly sales of Premium Bonds, at over £334m. With the total investment increasing by 25% in just one year, the chances of winning a Premium Bond Prize are at their lowest since 1979. The odds are fixed again, at 19,000–1. The number of prizes rises in line with the number of eligible units.

Tony Blair's Labour government takes power.

Chancellor, Gordon Brown, gives the Bank of England sole responsibility for setting interest rates to meet the Government's stated inflation target of 2.5%.

Diana, Princess of Wales, dies in a Paris car crash.

The Deep Blue chess program (IBM) beats the world chess champion, Garry Kasparov.

First *I'm Alan Partridge* TV series.

1998

July sees another record sales month, at over £384m. Total investments pass £10bn, a rise of 22%. ERNIE is now dispensing more than 500,000 prizes each month and the chances of winning a prize are now better at 19,000–1.

The Premium Bonds prize-checker is introduced on the National Savings website to help Bond holders trace unclaimed prizes. Premium Bonds forms can now be downloaded.

Prudential Banking is renamed Egg, becoming the UK's first internet bank

First airing of the game show, *Who Wants to be a Millionaire, The Royle Family* and Victoria Wood's *Dinnerladies*.

1999

National Savings outsources operations to Siemens Business Services, cutting its payroll from over 4,000 to around 130 – the biggest ever transfer of staff from the civil service to the private sector.

National Savings is the second-largest savings institution in the UK, looking after one-ninth of the nation's non-risk personal savings – the equivalent of £1,100 for every man, woman and child in the country.

The rate of growth of total Premium Bond investment is slowing, 16% up on the year. UK inflation is now down to 1.1%. The Prize Fund Rate is now down to 3.25% but the chances of winning a prize are longer, and now fixed again, at 24,000–1.

The Prize Fund is allocated 10% to higher value (£5,000 to £1m); 10% to medium (£500 and £1,000); 80% to lower value prizes (£50 and £100).

ISAs, the tax-free accounts replacing personal equity plans (PEPs) and tax-exempt special savings accounts (TESSAs), go on sale. NS&I launches a Cash Mini-ISA, backed up by a TV advertising campaign.

Ray Kurzweil's book, *The Age of Spiritual Machines*, predicts that machines with human-like Intelligence will be available from affordable computing devices within a couple of decades.

The first *Bremner, Bird and Fortune* TV series.

2000
As the dotcom bubble bursts and fears of recession grow, the Premium Bond growth rate slows to 10%. National Savings increases the Prize Fund Rate to 4.25%, with 690,000 monthly prizes worth £49m. With more prizes at all levels, the odds of winning are shortened to 22,000–1, then to 20,000–1.

238 year old Equitable Life Assurance Society nearly collapses, forcing it to cut pensions and retirement savings of its policyholders to stay afloat.

Alan Sugar is knighted for his contributions to business.

46 years on, GCHQ finally reveals the final secrets of the cipher and cryptanalysis that formed the essence of Colossus, the wartime code breaking computer, which formed the basis for ERNIE.

The Millennium Dome exhibition in London opens on 1st January and runs to 31st December.

The first run of *Da Ali G Show*.

2001
ERNIE's monthly prizes are now worth more than £750,000. October sees record monthly sales figures of over £403m. The total number of Premium Bond holders has actually fallen to 22.9 million, but the amount invested reaches £17bn and the average holding is up to £736.

The UK inflation rate is running at 1.8% and the Prize Fund Rate drops gradually from 4.25% to 3.25%. The odds of winning slip from to 20,000–1 to 24,000–1.

Tony Blair's Labour government wins a second term in office.

Sir Alan Budd delivers a report on the urgent need for reform of the burgeoning gambling industry, foreseeing a time soon when "Las Vegas comes to Leicester."

The Home Office is stripped of its responsibility for gambling, now taken up by the Department of Culture, Media and Sport, which also acquires responsibility for the National Lottery. Camelot retains its National Lottery licence against Richard Branson's "People's Lottery" bid.

The first TV episodes of *The Office* and Peter Kay's *Phoenix Nights*.

Comedy show, *Little Britain*, first airs on BBC Radio 4. "Yeah, I know."

2002
January sees a new record monthly Premium Bonds sales figure, £433m. In February, National Savings rebrands itself as National Savings & Investments (NS&I), replacing the crown motif with the conker and introducing a simple, clear and optimistic image. NS&I begins sponsorship of Classic FM Breakfast Show.

Peter Bareau retires in September and Alan Cook takes over as Chief Exec. 90% of NS&I products are still sold through local Post Office branches. Some NS&I products can be bought online but not Premium Bonds. But the NS&I website now allows Premium Bond holders to check for prizes won in last six months.

Queen Elizabeth II's Golden Jubilee is celebrated.

Bruce Forsyth is voted Greatest UK Game Show Host of All Time.

2003
The maximum investment is raised to £30,000 in May and NS&I achieves record Premium Bond sales of £1.1bn in the month. The total investment in Premium Bonds reaches £20bn, up 25% on the year.

Premium Bonds sales take off, ERNIE awards his 100 millionth Premium Bond prize and NS&I runs the "Unlocking Britain's Best Kept Secret" campaign.

The Government publishes its draft bill on tightening up gambling regulations, aimed at cleaning up a rapidly deregulating global industry and protecting children.

Little Britain debuts on TV. "Yeah, but, no, but."

2004
The UK inflation rate is running at 3.1% and the Premium Bond Prize Fund averages 2.7%. With so many Bonds in the draw, the odds of winning are down to 30,000–1 in April.

ERNIE 3 gives way to ERNIE 4, who appears in a public launch at London's Science Museum, alongside his three previous incarnations. ERNIE now gives out one million monthly prizes and the total investment reaches £25bn.

Premium Bonds are now available by telephone to the general public on 0500 007 007. Existing customers can now buy Premium Bonds by standing order, with a minimum purchase of £50.

NS&I launches its new website and closes the Ordinary Account, its original savings account from 1861, believed to be the oldest account in the UK, replacing it with the Easy Access Savings Account.

NS&I wins the DBA Design Effectiveness Award for its modern, user-friendly website.

NS&I begins sponsorship of The Classical BRIT Awards.

An East Londoner with a £17 Premium Bond holding bought in 1959, scoops a £1m prize.

The Catherine Tate Show debuts on TV. "Am I bovvered?"

The *Daily Mail* runs its "Kill the Casino" campaign, featuring Culture Secretary, Tessa Jowell, dressed as a croupier.

2005

Customers can finally buy Premium Bonds online at *www.nsandi.com* and all monthly prizes are published on the website. There are now two monthly Premium Bond jackpots of £1m. Premium Bonds now account for a third of all the money invested in NS&I. For the first time since 1982, the number of Premium Bond holders increases – to 23.1 million. To cope with growing demand, NS&I opens a new call centre in Glasgow.

SINGER KATHERINE JENKINS LAUNCHES THE DOUBLE JACKPOT AT THE SAVOY

PREMIUM BONDS

NS&I opens up a media centre in Blackpool to showcase ERNIE – welcome to the ERNIE simulator.

NS&I sponsors a show garden at Chelsea Flower Show.

Millionaire entrepreneur, Sir Alan Sugar, stars in the TV series, *The Apprentice*. Premium Bonds launches its first TV advertising campaign in six years, featuring Sir Alan Sugar.

A Hampshire woman scoops £1m on the shortest investment in Premium Bond history.

Tony Blair wins a third term in office.

The return of *Doctor Who* to TV screens after a 16-year absence.

Noel Edmonds makes his return as TV show host in *Deal or No Deal*.

The average 65-year-old man can expect to live another 19 years, until 84. For women, it's 87.

The term "chav" first appears in English dictionaries, a derogatory term for an ignorant subcultural stereotype with no respect for society, obsessed with jewellery and designer clothing.

2006

In October, the British public responds to the call to buy Bonds for the big 50th anniversary draw featuring five £1m prizes – with £2.2bn in sales in this month alone. For the second year in succession, the number of Premium Bond Holders is up – 23.6 million Premium Bond holders now have £33bn. Premium Bonds account for over 40% of the £73.4bn invested in NS&I, a 7% rise over the previous year. ERNIE is handing out over 1.25 million prizes a month. Year-on-year sales increase by 16%. The average holding is £1,405.

The UK inflation rate is running at 2.4% and the Prize Fund rate averages 3.25%. The chances of winning a Premium Bond prize are kept steady at 24,000–1.By the end of 2006, ERNIE has dispensed over 146 million prizes in his lifetime, worth £9.2bn.

Following new Home Office guidelines, prisoners can now buy Premium Bonds while behind bars.

When Alan Cook leaves to take over the reins at The Post Office, he has managed to reduce the amount of NS&I products sold through The Post Office to 62%.

Trevor Bayley acts as Chief Executive until Jane Platt comes on board.

NS&I's new Direct ISA soon tops the savings charts.

BBC PROMS IN THE PARK

NS&I sponsors BBC Proms in the Park and launches the 50th anniversary of Premium Bonds.

NS&I wins several awards including Most Effective Advertising Campaign and Tim Mack is voted Financial Services Marketer of the Year for the Sir Alan Sugar ads.

Gordon Brown announces the restoration of index-linked state pensions for 2012.

In its Pensions Bill, the Government proposes to raise the state pension age to 68 by 2050.

25% of Britons want to see cash abolished, according to research commissioned by the European Security Transport Association.

UK Christmas hamper firm, Farepak, goes bust. Thousands of thrifty people lose their annual savings.

First airing of all female TV sketch series, *Tittybangbang*.

2007

The UK inflation rate is up to 4.2% and the Premium Bond Prize Fund rate is 3.6%. The chances of winning a Prize are kept at 24,000–1. ERNIE is dispensing over 1.4 million tax-free prizes every month. 23.6 million people hold Premium Bonds worth over £35bn.

Over 1 billion people worldwide are using the Internet.

Manchester wins the nomination for the supercasino, ahead of the Dome in London and Blackpool. But the House of Lords rejects it.

Helen Mirren, wins an Oscar for her portrayal of Queen Elizabeth II, in the film *The Queen*.

In March, the international stock market crashes unexpectedly amid fears over the Chinese economy, wiping off all of last year's growth in a couple of days, before recovering.

Maestro, Mastercard's debit brand, declares "war on cash," running an ad campaign for a cashless society.

Last of the Summer Wine begins its 28th TV series, the longest-running comedy series in the world.

Sir Alan Sugar celebrates his 60th birthday, ranked 71st in the *Sunday Times* Rich List, with an estimated fortune of around £800m.

Tony Blair resigns as Prime Minister and makes way for the Chancellor of the Exchequer, Gordon Brown. Just like 50 years ago, in 1957, when Sir Anthony Eden gave way to Harold Macmillan.

In June, NS&I celebrates 50 years since the first Premium Bonds draw by creating five £1million winners.

50 YEARS ON, IN TRAFALGAR SQUARE...

ERNEST ACKNOWLEDGMENTS

I met ERNIE. I met Agent Million. There are many other people from the world of Premium Bonds, both present and historical, with whom I would like to have spoken, but time did not permit.

Here and now, however, I'm going to have to thank a few million people...

First, from National Savings & Investments: Mark Brooks, Head of Media and PR; Sue Simpson, Head of Brand; Tim Mack, Head of Marketing and Communications; Vicky Heron, Customer Insight Team; Sally Swait, Premium Bond Manager; Gill Stephens, Press Office. From Siemens: Nigel Laing, Operations Delivery Manager; Stuart Pilkington, Prizes Brand Supervisor; Lesley Scott, Team Leader, Customer Information Centre. Not forgetting Agent Million and, of course, ERNIE himself.

Jim Northover, founder of Lloyd Northover, had the idea for this book in the first place and gave me a fascinating insight into both the Premium Bonds and National Savings & Investments brands. Thanks, Jim. You brought it alive for me. Jim's colleagues, Emily Jones and Lavinia Young, were very resourceful in my quest for the right pictures – all featured here with permission of NS&I – and the editing process. Thanks to you, too.

I'd like to thank my family, friends and business associates for their wonderful contributions, especially: Craig Dearden-Phillips; Andy Sellers; Barnaby Benson; Catherine Hampshire; Chris Hoskins; Clare Moore; James Harkness; Lisa Betteridge; Matt Bellamy; Sally Langley; Simon Harrop; Zoe Hazelden; Bill Spence; Adam Billiald; Chris Murphy; Fiona Pearce; Jayne McGann; Jo Ball; John Grounds; Tim Parr; Viki Bell; Yanni Bourtsouklis; Chris Byron; Katy Sewell; Patrick Ballin; Tom Eilfield; Pete Neville; Sue D.

Many thanks go to my publishers at Cyan Books, Martin Liu and Pom Somkabcharti for their commission and belief that I could deliver this independent book in the impossibly short timeframe available.

I appreciate the way Damian Mullan has designed this book, combining elements of Premium Bonds branding with the spirit of the text. Thanks, Damian.

My thanks go to Mintel and Ipsos Mori for use of their research and statistics.

Last, but not least, there would have been no point in writing this book without saying thank you to every Premium Bond holder. All 23 million of you. I couldn't have done it without you.

And I certainly couldn't have done it without the editing patience of my brilliant and inspiring wife and life support system, Debbie. Thank you, again.

OTHER GREAT BRAND STORIES

ADIDAS *All Day I Dream About Sport: The story of the adidas brand* by Conrad Brunner

ARSENAL *Winning Together: The story of the Arsenal brand* by John Simmons & Matt Simmons

BANYAN TREE *A Brand Born of Romance* by Andy Milligan

BECKHAM *The Story of How Brand Beckham was Built* by Andy Milligan

DYSON *The Domestic Engineer: How Dyson changed the meaning of cleaning* by Iain Carruthers

eBAY *The Story of a Brand that Taught Millions of People to Trust One Another* by Elen Lewis

GOOGLE *Search Me: The surprising success of Google* by Neil Taylor

GUINNESS *Guinness is Guinness: The colourful story of a black and white brand* by Mark Griffiths

HARRY POTTER *Wizard!: Harry Potter's brand magic* by Stephen Brown

IKEA *A Brand for All the People* by Elen Lewis

INNOCENT *Building a Brand from Nothing but Fruit* by John Simmons

SCOTCH WHISKY *Creative Fire: The story of Scotland's greatest export* by Stuart Delves

STARBUCKS *My Sister's a Barista: How they made Starbucks a home away from home* by John Simmons

UNITED STATES *Brand America: The mother of all brands* by Simon Anholt & Jeremy Hildreth